Childhood, Education and Philosophy

This book explores the idea of a childlike education and offers critical tools to question traditional forms of education, and alternative ways to understand and practice the relationship between education and childhood. Engaging with the work of Michel Foucault, Jacques Rancière, Giorgio Agamben and Simón Rodríguez, it contributes to the development of a philosophical framework for the pedagogical idea at the core of the book, that of a childlike education.

Divided into two parts, the book introduces innovative ideas through philosophical argument and discussion, challenging existing understandings of what it means to teach or to form a child, and putting into question the idea of education as a process of formation. The first part of the book consists of a dialogue with a number of interlocutors in order to develop an original conception of education. The second part presents the idea of a childlike education, beginning with a discussion of the relationships between childhood and philosophy, and followed by a critique of the place of philosophical experience in a childhood of education.

Instead of asking how philosophy might educate childhood, this book raises the question of how childhood might educate philosophy. It will be of key value to researchers, educators and postgraduate students in the fields of education and the human sciences.

Walter Kohan is Professor of Philosophy of Education at the State University of Rio de Janeiro, Brazil. He is also a Researcher at the National Council of Scientific and Technological Research of Brazil (CNPQ) and the Carlos Chagas Filho Research Support Foundation (FAPERJ), and was previously President of the International Council of Philosophical Inquiry with Children (ICPIC).

New directions in the philosophy of education series

Series Editors: Michael A. Peters
University of Waikato, New Zealand; University of Illinois, USA
Gert Biesta
University of Luxembourg, Luxembourg

This book series is devoted to the exploration of new directions in the philosophy of education. After the linguistic turn, the cultural turn, and the historical turn, where might we go? Does the future promise a digital turn with a greater return to connectionism, biology, and biopolitics based on new understandings of system theory and knowledge ecologies? Does it foreshadow a genuinely alternative radical global turn based on a new openness and interconnectedness? Does it leave humanism behind or will it reengage with the question of the human in new and unprecedented ways? How should philosophy of education reflect new forces of globalization? How can it become less Anglo-centric and develop a greater sensitivity to other traditions, languages, and forms of thinking and writing, including those that are not rooted in the canon of Western philosophy but in other traditions that share the 'love of wisdom' that characterizes the wide diversity within Western philosophy itself. Can this be done through a turn to intercultural philosophy? To indigenous forms of philosophy and philosophizing? Does it need a post-Wittgensteinian philosophy of education? A postpostmodern philosophy? Or should it perhaps leave the whole construction of 'post'-positions behind?

In addition to the question of the intellectual resources for the future of philosophy of education, what are the issues and concerns that philosophers of education should engage with? How should they position themselves? What is their specific contribution? What kind of intellectual and strategic alliances should they pursue? Should philosophy of education become more global, and if so, what would the shape of that be? Should it become more cosmopolitan or perhaps more decentred? Perhaps most importantly in the digital age, the time of the global knowledge economy that reprofiles education as privatized human capital and simultaneously in terms of an historic openness, is there a philosophy of education that grows out of education itself, out of the concerns for new forms of teaching, studying, learning and speaking that can provide comment on ethical and epistemological configurations of economics and politics of knowledge? Can and should this imply a reconnection with questions of democracy and justice?

This series comprises texts that explore, identify and articulate new directions in the philosophy of education. It aims to build bridges, both geographically and temporally: bridges across different traditions and practices and bridges towards a different future for philosophy of education.

In this series

On Study
Giorgio Agamben and educational potentiality
Tyson E. Lewis

Education, Experience and Existence
Engaging Dewey, Peirce and Heidegger
John Quay

African Philosophy of Education Reconsidered
On being human
Yusef Waghid

Buber and Education
Dialogue as conflict resolution
W. John Morgan and Alexandre Guilherme

Henri Lefebvre and Education
Space, history, theory
Sue Middleton

Thomas Jefferson's Philosophy of Education
Autopian dream
M. Andrew Holowchak

Edusemiotics
Semiotic philosophy as educational foundation
Andrew Stables and Inna Semetsky

Childhood, Education and Philosophy
New ideas for an old relationship
Walter Kohan

Between Truth and Freedom
Rousseau and our contemporary political and educational culture
Kenneth Wain

Childhood, Education and Philosophy

New ideas for an old relationship

Walter Kohan

Routledge
Taylor & Francis Group

LONDON AND NEW YORK

First published 2015
by Routledge

2 Park Square, Milton Park, Abingdon, Oxon OX14 4RN
711 Third Avenue, New York, NY 10017, USA

Routledge is an imprint of the Taylor & Francis Group, an informa business

First issued in paperback 2017

British Library Cataloguing in Publication Data
A catalogue record for this book is available from the British Library

Library of Congress Cataloging-in-Publication Data
Kohan, Walter Omar.
Childhood, education, and philosophy : new ideas for an old
relationship / Walter Kohan.
pages cm – (New directions in the philosophy of education)
1. Education–Philosophy. 2. Children and philosophy. I. Title.
LB14.7.K65 2015
370.1–dc23
2014022327

ISBN: 978-1-138-78797-1 (hbk)
ISBN: 978-1-138-71298-0 (pbk)

Typeset in Bembo
by Cenveo Publisher Services

3/13/18

To my mother Marta, to my father Isaac.
To the pride and joy they would have
experienced if they had read this book.

Contents

Series editors' foreword

Walter Omar Kohan's book, *Childhood, Education and Philosophy: New ideas for an old relationship,* takes three very familiar terms—childhood, education, and philosophy—and turns them inside out, so to speak, so that they lose their familiarity and put us in a position where we can think again about what they mean, individually and in connection. This is a major achievement and a major contribution to the field of philosophy of education and educational scholarship more widely, because the terms that are closest to what our work is about often tend to escape critical scrutiny; they become all too familiar. In "returning" these key terms to the field of philosophy of education Kohan exemplifies one of the key ideas of his book, namely that of an education that is childlike. Such an education does not seek to form childhood, as he puts it, but rather seeks to make education childlike. Such a childlike education is close to how Kohan approaches philosophy itself, that is, not as an avenue towards knowledge and truth, but as a process of questioning and unlearning what we know and affirming the value of not knowing, of attempting to respond to those questions which cannot be answered. Kohan develops his ideas about a childlike education in conversation with a number of philosophers and educators. In the first part of the book he goes in discussion with Rancière/Jacotot, Foucault, and Rodríguez in order, so we might say, to clear the terrain. In the second part of the book this allows him to put forward his case for a childlike education, again in discussion with a number of thinkers but ultimately "staging" the argument through the work of Plato and Socrates. Kohan's argument is not just intellectual—there is clearly "at stake", which is not only visible in the chapters that form the more formal part of the book, but also in the two conversations that "frame" the book, one at the beginning and one at the end. Here we can not only see Kohan's thinking "at work", but we can also see a particular quality of his writing, that is, his ability to "think-with", in conversation or correspondence, as it is called in the Afterword. Kohan invites his readers not to see his book as a truth-to-be-accepted, but as a book that allows its readers, and perhaps even requires from its readers, to establish different relationships to its content. There is therefore work to be done by the readers of this book through which they might well experience the very different understandings of childhood, education and philosophy that the book is also about.

Gert Biesta and Michael A. Peters
June 2014

Presentation

Michel Foucault (1994/1978: 43 ff.) distinguished between two kinds of books, or two kinds of relationships to the reading of a book: books as experience and books as truth. Simply stated, when one writes a book under the logic of truth it is because, as an author, she or he thinks that they are in possession of a given truth. The meaning and sense of their writing is thus derived through the transmission of that truth to the readers of their book.

Differently, when a book is written under the logic of experience certain truths are also affirmed, but they are not affirmed in order to be transmitted, but rather to put our relationship to them into question. Thus the logic of truth and the logic of experience are in a certain dimension opposed, the latter being a way of putting into question the former, both by writers and readers. If writers of book-truths establish and transmit a truth, writers and readers of book-experience put into question both the truths that the book affirms and their relationship to those truths. This particular book aspires to be a case of book-experience, written under the logic of experience and calling for reader-experience. It is a book about childhood, philosophy and education, which provokes a reading and thinking-through of what we mean by a philosophical education of childhood. It puts into question, through philosophy and education, truths concerning childhood and our relationship to those truths. In other words, it is a book that affirms childhood as experience and at the same time experiences childhood as both philosophy and education.

Childhood, in its philosophical and educational dimension, is then at the core of this experience of writing. The first part of the book presents some interlocutors (Jacques Rancière, Michel Foucault—with Socrates and the Cynics—and Simón Rodríguez) who put into question the way we connect childhood, philosophy and education. Significantly, childhood does not appear as a direct content or as a theme in this section of the book, but it is at the core of my text, in that a kind of childhood of philosophy and/as/or education flows through the entire section. These three chapters are focused on the lives of three teachers, professors, and educators. In "Teaching as verification of equality: Jacques Rancière and *The Ignorant Schoolmaster*" I problematize the paradigm that conceptualizes education as the formation/emancipation of childhood. I do so by criticizing the role of explanation in education from an emancipatory perspective, as it was offered by Joseph Jacotot between the last decades of the eighteenth century and the first part of the nineteenth century. Nevertheless, even though Jacotot's conception of a teacher supports an emancipatory perspective, it considers it impossible for a teacher to be an emancipator, at least by the same logic according to which she is a teacher. Following this path, there seems to be no place, according to Rancière, for an emancipatory school—no possibility of emancipation among social institutions. "What then can we educate for?" and "Why and for what are we educating childhood if emancipation is not possible among social institutions?" are some of the questions that arise in this chapter. "The teaching of the courage of living in Socrates and the Cynics: Michel Foucault" focuses on Foucault's last courses at the Collège de France, specifically on the Greek notion of *parrhesia*—that is, "frank speech"—to tell the truth. In this context, Socrates and the Cynics are of crucial importance. Socrates has a particular place here in that he reframes the meaning and sense of being a teacher: while traditional teachers in Athens considered the main aim of teaching to be the transmission of their knowledge to those who didn't have it, Socrates emphasized leading others to "take care" of themselves—of what up until then they were not taking care of. Socrates does not provide a model of education as transmission or formation, but rather as Caring or De-forming or Transforming. The Cynics radicalized the Socratic model of the teacher by offering their lives as the only testimony a teacher can offer. For the Cynics their manner of life is their truth.

The third chapter of this section, "Journeying as a way of living, endeavors: Simón Rodríguez" presents this Venezuelan pedagogue as a figure who echoes Jacototian and Socratic-Cynic perspectives of the educator as a philosopher. Rodríguez affirms a direct, informal discursive style, a nomadic and iconoclastic manner of life, an emphasis on the role of attention in education, and on the crucial importance of popular education in Latin America. Special attention is given in this chapter to his motto "We invent or we err". Together, these three educational dimensions—the Socratic-Cynic, the Jacototian and Rodriguezian—provide key elements of the foundation on which the second part of the book is built, which queries the notion of a "childlike education", and what that means for an educator as philosopher, or a philosopher as educator. All three illustrate what it means not only to think but to practice and to live a childlike education. A "new" reading or reconstruction of the figure of Socrates underlies these three chapters—one from his critic Jacques Rancière, another in the apology by Michel Foucault, and another in his re-birth as the "Socrates of Caracas", Simón Rodríguez.

The second part of this book focuses on the idea of childhood. "Philosophy and childhood: Possibilities of an encounter" explores differently the ways in which philosophy and childhood encounter each other. It discusses the field known as "philosophy of childhood" and the place given to children and childhood in the educational program known as "philosophy for children".

A proposal for an alternative relationship between childhood and philosophy is also included in this section. "Childhood, education and philosophy: Notes on deterritorialization" argues that education might be practiced under a different logic than the logic of education-as-the-formation-of-childhood. As such, it puts into question the traditional cultural and psychological practice of considering children as representing adults' opportunities to impose their own ideals on children, and challenges the notion that education is an appropriate instrument for such ends. More specifically, it considers how the purposes of practicing philosophy with children might be considered to be more than a practice that serves the dominant social and political institutions of childhood. In this chapter ancient (Heraclitus) and contemporary (Deleuze, Lyotard) philosophical contributions are offered in order to think of new concepts and vocabularies for childhood. An example of the deterritorialization of the relation between childhood and education is given in the description of a practical project undertaken in public schools in the environs of Rio de Janeiro. This project affirms a strong emphasis on the concept of the "experience of philosophical thinking". The figure of a "childlike teacher" is offered here, constructed along the lines of the Socratic archetype that is traced in the first part of the book.

Finally, "Plato and Socrates: From educator of childhood to childlike educator?" deals with the distinction between two forms of education—the Platonic and the Socratic—that have been present throughout all previous chapters. The former educates childhood with a goal of transforming what is into what it ought to be. The latter does not seek to form childhood, but to make education childlike. In order to unpack the philosophical and pedagogical dimensions of this opposition, the first part of the chapter highlights the way in which philosophy is presented indirectly in some of Plato's *dialogues*, beginning with Phaedrus' characterization of Socrates as the most extraordinary of all Athenians, without a place and unfamiliar (*atopotatos*)—someone who, although he never ventured beyond the city limits, appears to behave like a foreigner (*xenagoumenoi*) in the *Phaedrus* (230c). The second part details Plato's condemnation of writing in the *Phaedrus*, and draws on the critique by Jacques Derrida and Gilles Deleuze in order to establish what is at stake in this condemnation. In the third part, the pedagogical and political implications of this condemnation are reviewed, and Plato is placed in a surprising position in relation to his own teacher, Socrates.

Two conversations with special interlocutors are included as a preface and an afterword. In a sense they are the core of this book, if it is to be appreciated not only or not mainly in its content but in its form. Both dialogues affirm an experience of thinking together with friends, *philodialogos,* in which the only thing that remains is the impossibility of thinking in the same way as at the beginning of our conversation-correspondence. The first dialogue, between David Kennedy and myself, offers a discussion of the meaning, sense and social function of school, both as an institution and as a time-space for the practice of *schole* (free-time, leisure). It also discusses the different types of

Greek time (*aion, kairos, chronos*) and the place of childhood in educational discourse. It is meant to inspire a questioning of the idea of childhood and its relationship to time and school. The Afterword, a dialogue with Jan Masschelein, is a correspondence on what it means to be a philosopher or/ and/as educator, which seeks to uncover (or invent) the terms and boundaries of a non-colonized politics for a (new) education yet to be thought and affirmed.

The chapters that compose this book have been written over a period of almost 15 years, starting with Chapter 4, an earlier version of "Philosophy and childhood: Possibilities of an encounter" prepared for the World Conference of Philosophy in Boston (EUA), 1998 and published in a previous version as "What Can Philosophy and Children Offer Each Other," *Thinking. The Journal of Philosophy for Children*, 12(2), 1999, 25–30. Some of the chapters (1–3) have been previously written and published in French, Spanish and Portuguese and slightly adapted for this book. Chapter 1 ("Teaching as verification of equality: Jacques Rancière and *The Ignorant Schoolmaster*") was originally published in French as "Rancière et l'éducation. Forces et limites – philosophiques et politiques – d'un antiprogressisme", in: *La Philosophie déplacée*. Autour de Jacques Rancière. Paris: Horleu, 2006, 212–24. Most of "The teaching of the courage of living in Socrates and the Cynics: Michel Foucault" was published in Portuguese in "Sócrates no último curso de Foucault", in: *Biopolítica, escola e resistência. Infâncias para a formação de professores*. Campinas, SP: Alínea, 2012, 103–17 and a Spanish version of "Journeying as a way of living, endeavors: Simón Rodríguez" was published in "En torno al pensamiento como nomadismo y a la vida como errancia. Entre Deleuze, Maffesoli y Rodríguez", *Ensayo y Error*. Revista de Educación y Ciencias Sociales, 21, 2012, 33–54. Previous versions of Chapters 5 and 6 were originally written and published in English: "Childhood, education and philosophy: Notes on deterritorialization" in *Journal of Philosophy of Education*, 45, 2011, 339–57, but here a special section on G. Agamben has been added to this chapter; with few changes, "Plato and Socrates: From an educator of childhood to a childlike educator?" was previously published in *Studies in Philosophy and Education*, 32, 2013, 313–25. The Preface is a Dialogue with David Kennedy originally presented as a Keynote Lecture to the XVII Conference of the International Council of Philosophical Inquiry with Children, at the University of Cape Town, South Africa, September 2013 and published in *Childhood & Philosophy*, 10, 19, 2014. The Afterword is an unpublished dialogue, with Jan Masschelein, which unfolded through email correspondence over the final months of 2013 and the beginning of 2014.

All writing is a result of many eyes, hands, ears and noses. This idea is particularly clear in the case of this text, and I would like to acknowledge and thank those who have been with me over the course of these years. First, I thank Argentinian Public Education, that allowed my formation in Philosophy at the University of Buenos Aires. I still recognize the thought of some of my Professors there—Conrado Eggers Lan and Victoria Juliá for example—in my own thinking. Second, I thank Brazilian Public Education, which has supported my research in the field of Philosophy of Education mainly through my position as Full Professor at the State University of Rio de Janeiro and as a researcher in foundations such as FAPERJ (Support to Research of the State of Rio de Janeiro) and CNPq (National Council of Scientific and Technological Research). Third, I thank my colleagues and students at the Center of Philosophical Studies on Childhood (NEFI) at the State University of Rio de Janeiro, who have through the last 12 years been highly motivating interlocutors of my ideas. I should also thank colleagues and friends from all over the world who have been decisive influences on this text: David Kennedy, an-other (my)self, (my)self in other, with whom I've written the Preface (and some other dialogues) has showed me from the very beginning of our relationship the various meanings of friendship; David has also corrected the English in some of these chapters, particularly Chapter 5 and the Afterword, and has always encouraged my writing and publication in English; Matthew Lipman and Ann Margaret Sharp opened the world of philosophical practices with childhood to me, out of which emerges Chapter 4; Joanna Haynes and Karin Murris invited me to write Chapter 6 (corrected by Simon Geschwindt) and have also inspired and encouraged my thinking and writing throughout the last years; Jason Wozniak has always been encouraging about the need to translate my writing into English. Stéphane Douailler and Hubert Vincent welcomed me in Paris during two semesters in the academic years between 2005 and 2007 and supported me in the process of writing Chapters 1 and 2. Gregorio Valera-Villegas introduced me to and has encouraged my reading of Simón Rodríguez, out of which emerges Chapter 3. And even if he is not explicitly present, my conversations with Giuseppe Ferraro are at the heart of this writing. The editors of this series, Gert Biesta and Michael Peters, have been very sensitive to this project and Gert Biesta has not only supported my project, but helped me to think through the structure and content of this book.

Less clearly but no less evidently, ideas and conversations with a number of friends in different countries have given inspiration and form to these pages in the course of the last decade. Among them, I would like to mention Abiel Santos, Ada Kroef, Adelaide Léo, Adriana Arpini, Adriana Fresquet, Adriana Passalia, Adriana Presentini, Adriana Maria Silva, Aimberé Quintiliano, Alejandra Walzer, Alejandro Cerletti, Alessandra Lopes, Alfredo Veiga-Neto, Alice Pessanha, Alicia Moreno, Alvaro Teixeira Ribeiro, Ana Corina Salas, Ana Flávia Teixera, André Martins, Andrea Benvenuto, Andrea Díaz, Andrea Quiroga, Andreia Bieri, Andrezza Amorelli, Anelice Ribetto, Angélica Sátiro, Antonio Cosentino, Aparecida Rodrigues, Arianne Hecker, Arleny Carpio, Arlindo Picoli, Arthur Arruda, Barbara Oliveira, Beatriz Gutiérrez Muller, Bernardina Leal, Bo Malmhester, Carla Almeida, Carlos Skliar, Carmen Sanches, Carmen Zavala, Carolina Fonseca, Carolina Seidel, Catarina

Dallapicula, César Leite, Christine Gehrett, Cielo Salviolo, Cintia Canedi, Claudia Márcico, Conceição Gislane Nóbrega, Cristina Rossi, Dagmar Mello e Silva, Dalva Garcia, Daniel Lesteime, Daniela Guimarães, Danilo Augusto Melo, David Sumiacher, Diego di Masi, Diego Pineda, Dirce Solis, Domenico Megu Chionetti, Donaji Lopez, Dora Ramirez, Edna Olimpia da Cunha, Eduardo Bustello, Elena Teresa José, Elisete Tomazetti, Ellen Parrela, Erasmo Valadão, Ester Heuser, Esther Grossi, Eugenio Echeverría, Eva Marsal, Fabiana Martins, Fabiana Olarieta, Fabiana Rassi, Félix García Moriyón, Fernando Bárcena, Filipe Ceppas, Flávia Marinho, Flávia Corrêa, Fulvio Manara, Gabriela Berti, Giovânia Costa, Guillermo Tagiaferri, Hannu Juuso, Hector Palma, Hélia Freitas, Homero Lima, Humberto Guido, Ingrid Müller Xavier, Jaime Vieyra, Jana Mohr Lone, Jason Wozniak, Ji Aeh Lee, Joana Tolentino, Jorge Larrosa, José García Molina, José Gondra, José Ricardo Santiago Júnior, Joseph Giordmania, Juan Pablo Álvarez Coronado, Julia Krüger, Juliana Merçon, Junot Cornélio Matos, Kaique Leones, Kátia Bizzo, Kátia Franca, Kelsiane Mattos, Lana Andrade, Laura Viviana Agratti, Laura de la Fuente, Laura Morales, Laurance Splitter, Lea Tiriba, Leila Riger, Leoni Maria Padilha Henning, Letícia Fonseca, Lígia Aquino, Liliana Guzman, Livio Rossetti, Lucia Helena Pulino, Luciana Kalil, Lucrecio Sa, Luis Ángel Castello, Marcelo Senna Guimarães, Marcos Lorieri, Maria Auxiliadora Máximo, María Elena Madrid, Maria Elena Merino, Maria Jacintha Vargas, María José Guzmán, Maria Luisa Oswald, Maria Reilta Dantas Cirino, María Teresa de La Garza, Maria Teresa Suarez, Mariana Alvarado, Mariana Ventrice, Mariela Avila, Marina Santi, Marines Dias, Mario Berrios, Maristela Barenco, Marlene Torrezan, Marta Atehortúa, Marta Elena Rita Vennera, Marta Vitória de Alencar, Maughn Gregory, Maura Striano, Mauricio Langón, Mauricio Rocha, Maximiliano Durán, Maximiliano López, Miguel Angel Barrenechea, Mirella Fant Alves, Monica Costa Netto, Myriam Southwell, Nadia Kennedy, Nair Tuboitti, Nicholas Go, Noria Fiezzi, Olga Grau, Oscar Pulido, Osvaldo Silva, Pablo de Vargas, Pablo Severiano Benevides, Paolo Vittoria, Patrice Vermeren, Patricia Hannam, Paula Gomes, Paula Helena Mateos, Paula Ramos, Pedro Gontijo, Pedro Lespada, Pedro Pagni, Philip Cam, Philip Guin, Pierpaolo Casarin, Priscila Campos Ribeiro, Priscilla dos Santos Moreira, Rafael Haddock-Lobo, Rafael Mello Barbosa, Rafaela Vieira, Ralph Bannell, Renato Noguera, Ricardo Sassone, Renê José Trentin Silveira, Rita Pedro, Rita Ribes, Robert Segal, Roberto Rondon, Rodolfo Rezola, Rogier Viegas, Ronai Rocha, Rosa Licata, Rosana Fernandes, Rosi Giordano, Rosimeri Dias, Rossana Cascudo, Roxana Ortín, Rudhra Gallina, Rui Mayer, Sandra Corazza, Sara Goering, Sarah Nery, Sérgio Carreira, Sérgio Sardi, Silvana Vignale, Silvia Bevilacqua, Silvia Rebgliati, Silvio Gallo, Simona Marino, Simone Tressi, Siomara Borba, Siomara Florez, Socorro Giménez, Solange Noronha, Stefano Oliverio, Sylvio Gadelha, Tainá Lopes, Tarcísio Pinto, Terada (San) Toshiro, Thomas E. Wartenberg, Tiago Ribeiro, Tuillang Yuing, Vanise Dutra Gomes, Vera Valdemarin, Vera Vasconcelos, Verónica Bethencourt, Vinicius Vicenzi, Waldênia Leão de Carvalho, Wanderson Flor Nascimento, Wendy Turgeon, Wilbert Tapia, Yolanda Perugini.

Only now I realize how lucky I've been to be in touch with so many wonderful people! Thanks to all, and to a number of others whom my memory is surely overlooking.

Walter Omar Kohan
Rio de Janeiro, April 2014

Preface

School and the future of *schole*: A preliminary dialogue with David Kennedy

WALTER OMAR KOHAN: We usually think about going to school, for example, to introduce philosophy in order to interfere in what school is doing, such as forming critical or creative citizens or to foster a kind of thinking that is not taking place there. We usually consider school as just there—we take its existence for granted, and we postulate some meanings and senses to introduce philosophy at that school. But maybe we can think about the relationship between philosophy (or whatever) and school differently. J. Rancière notes in an essay called "School, production, equality" (1988) that in its origin, as in the Greek *schole*, the school was a place of separation of two different uses or experiences of time: inside the school, the experience of those who have free-time, time for leisure, for learning, for studying, time to lose or to experience for itself and not for any other thing outside the experience itself. Outside school, the experience of productive time, of those who employ their time because of what they can obtain out of it. In this sense, in relation to time, all are equal inside school, they have the same experience of time—the experience of a student, of being a student. It is clear that in our time schools are very far from that. Quite the contrary, nearly everything in school is done because of what can be obtained from it outside of school. Schools prepare us for the labor market, the university, the future and so on—for many things but not so much for school itself—it seems as if there is no more *schole* in schools. In this sense, we can think that philosophy might go to school to restore this school (as *schole*) that does not exist any more. In other words, not assuming that the school is there, but in order that the school that is there could be a school-as-*schole*. What do you think about this idea?

DAVID KENNEDY: I think that the time of *schole* is in fact the time of childhood itself in the sense of what Winnicott (1971) called "transitional space", and what you have called, after Heraclitus (2001, fr. 52), "*aion*" as opposed to *chronos* and *kairos*, three Greek terms for different qualities of time. Transitional space is the space in which the subject-object relation and hence the "real" and the "imagined" are not fixed and codified in any one cultural or historical form. As such it is the space of the virtual—of creativity and deep play of various sorts, including the deep play of philosophical inquiry. It is a space in which the child as polymorph thrives. It is the space of the subject-object relation "identity-with", which Northrup Frye (1947), in his analysis of William Blake's *Songs of innocence* , designates as "not merely a creative state ... but also a moral state corresponding to the older state of innocence, which traditionally has been associated with the child: the sense that the child in particular responds to his surroundings to the point of identifying with them" (236). Another way of thinking *schole* is to understand it as a "brain-shelter", invented by the species in the interest of personal and collective transformation. By this I mean that the human brain is characterized by a high level of plasticity, that brain growth continues for the first 22 years of life, and that the neurological pathways that we develop are shaped by the experience we have. The particular wiring that we end up with is a product of the experience of the first 22 years. *Schole*, I would suggest, is the shelter from what you call "productive time", which tends to shut down transitional space in the interests of survival and therefore of efficiency and what Blake called "single vision", and shuts down brain growth by pushing intentionality downward to the lower brain, the amygdala, which deals with perceived threat, and thus governs fight or flight or freeze response, in perceived "life or death" decisions, whether they are or not. In the brain shelter of *schole* we have the "leisure" to allow new patterns, new connections, new values and centers of meaning. But how can philosophy restore this space in a moribund institutional culture, corrupted by surplus repression, commodification and the simulacrum? Sometimes philosophy seems to me to be mainly a destructive force in our time: it takes things apart and cannot put them back together again. How do you understand philosophy anyway?

WOK: That's an interesting connection between *schole* and *aion* through childhood. And I agree that philosophy sometimes seems to be placed as an obstacle to *schole* and *aion*. But philosophy is multiple, diverse ... and philosophy is also an experience of thinking in *aion*. I mean, philosophy plays the thinking game in aionic time, at least when played as the lived experience of putting one's own life into question, in a tradition as old as Socrates. I know philosophy is actually also practiced in very different ways, and the picture I've just drawn might sound ridiculous or even dangerous to many professional philosophers of our time, but it also sounded like that in Socrates' time, and it will probably will always continue to sound like that to some. In fact it is really challenging to think about the possibilities of any aionic experience of thinking in institutions as overwhelmed by chronological time as ours are. How to initiate it is not a simple question to answer but in actual fact it's a matter of practice and exercise. It is true that the context seems completely hostile. But if on the one hand this seems to be extremely negative, on the other hand the less aionic thinking seems possible, the more necessary it becomes. And philosophy has also this dimension of thinking and doing the impossible—again, at least since Socrates. It might be dangerous or considered stupid and nonsensical, but it is always possible. It is just a matter of practice—of seeing how it goes and what its effects are. But I am not sure I really answered your question. How would you yourself answer your question?

DK: Maybe I can get at a tentative answer to my own question by trying a genealogical approach to the arguments, popular among some, *against* the practice of community of philosophical inquiry (CPI) in schools. First, from the Left: 1) It's socialization into a "white", "western", rationalistic, normalizing discourse, the very discourse of the colonizers, and implicitly ignores or suppresses alternative discourses; 2) It is reduced to a program for "critical thinking", one more skill useful for adjusting to the workplace and the political status quo; 3) It trivializes the very values it seeks to explore by implicitly taking a "values clarification" approach to key philosophical concepts, starting from the assumption that everybody has their own emotionally rooted opinion which they have a perfect right to, etc., thus promoting a false kind of tolerance. And from the Right: 1) It intrudes upon and interferes with the indoctrination-rights of the family; 2) By problematizing deep concepts, it erodes those fundamental beliefs that are the basis for our common morality, and discredits a religious approach to belief, which is based on faith and modest acceptance of an authoritative view, not questioning; 3) To the extent that the school represents the state, CPI amounts to government ideological imposition; 4) It is a waste of productive time to deliberate about concepts that make no difference to the way the world works, or at best breed discontent: it is, in other words, an offense against The Market; 5) It alienates the youth by systematically practicing a sort of doubt that can cripple motivation and the healthy innocence of the young; 6) It foments potential social and political rebellion.

Now it seems to me that your implicit definition of philosophy as the practice of "thinking in aionic time", and of "thinking and doing the impossible", or "unexpectable", might elude all these criticisms, but I am not exactly sure how. Most obvious is the setting up of a wall between "free" and "productive" time—something of an artificial wall, it could be argued (after all, can we really separate *homo faber* and *homo ludens*?). Then, we can say, behind that wall, in that shelter from productive time, who knows what sort of new brain can emerge—given that, following Spinoza (1996), "No one has yet determined what a body can do from the laws of Nature alone" (71). Perhaps another clue is the identification of philosophy with art, which is the more traditional location of *aion* and the unexpectable. Perhaps the form of philosophy you are contemplating is a form of self-making, which begins as a process of "putting one's own life into question", whereby one's own life becomes a work of art. But what strikes me now is that the image of philosophy that this suggests is different from, not just the traditional one, but even from our notion of philosophy as a communal dialogical practice—that is, CPI. It seems to suggest that we don't bring philosophy to school to make it into *schole*, but rather *schole* as a form of lived experience is inherently philosophical. This suggests further that *schole is already there* in any given community of humans, it is immanent and emergent, it waits below the surface to rise into speech and act.

WOK: Let me consider the critiques, beginning with the ones from the Right. The first assumes an interesting understanding of the aims of philosophy: yes, surely philosophical questioning "intrudes upon and interferes with the indoctrination-rights of the family" and not only those of the family. It's difficult to see a more important task than this one, particularly in our time—if, that is, we want to live an examined and not a dogmatic life. The second, which is very close to the first one, also realizes that for philosophy there is no absolute or unquestionable value or belief, either moral or religious. The third one needs to be confronted with some distinctions between state and government, school and philosophy, ideology and politics: philosophy is a political force in a state institution than can put into question all (ideological) impositions, even from governments. The fourth critique from the Right suggests a celebration: yes! Philosophy *is* a waste of productive time and a saving of free or aionic time, affirming another kind of life than a producer-consumer life. Critique number five should be taken seriously in that philosophy is a sort of innocent practice (in the sense that it has no other intention than philosophical questioning itself) that can at the same time deconstruct childish innocence and introduce some kind of lack, or some form of pandemonium. Finally, the Right is right, this is what it is all about: philosophical rebellion which in itself is a political rebellion, most probably not in the sense of the Right but in that after philosophy there is no way to continue living the way we were living in the polis.

The Left's critiques look more interesting. It is true that philosophy has been practiced as a form of domination through "white", "western", "rationalistic", "normalizing", and "colonizing" discourses, but it has also been practiced in the opposite way through the discourse of the "other", "anti-colonialist", "anti-hegemonic" and so on. So the question is controversial inside philosophy itself. Second, if understood as a program for "critical thinking"—which in fact is the case in many instances—then I would agree that it is a practice of little interest, which could be useful for the political status quo. Third, the so-called "values clarification" approach seems to me something very different from philosophy, or at most a very small aspect of it. By that I mean that if we just clarify values we might as well not do philosophy. It is clearly not enough. In fact, tolerance, just like any other value, is an object of philosophical genealogical critique and not an aim in itself. Of course, critics may be not satisfied with these answers and other critiques could be put, but then we would still be in the realm of that form of philosophy we have already entered. And yes, I think the form of philosophy I am developing is "a form of self-making", which begins as a process of "putting one's own life into question", whereby one's own life becomes a work of art. You have put it in very nice words! There are many interesting concepts here to think about, like the self-making form, where self can be something very soft and diverse and the "making" process could be a kind of imaginative way of living. But I do not see this form of philosophy as in conflict with communal dialogical practice. It all depends on how we think about this self-making or inventing process that could be dialogical and communal. Don't you think so? And I also love your idea of making a verb out of the noun or an action out of the substance *schole*. There is nothing more inspiring and inviting to philosophy. But maybe school does not in fact inherently resist this form of philosophy. Or would? What do you think?

DK: Which comes first—school or *schole*? Are the two forms of community and temporality antipathetic? I would like to suggest that school and *schole* emerge from the same evolutionary impulse, which is to establish a zone in the culture which is set apart for purposes of transformation. Before the creation of that separated space, we seem to have what David Lancy, in his magisterial work *The Anthropology of Childhood* (2008) calls the "village" or the "chore" curriculum, characteristic of pre-industrial societies. Here, education is folded seamlessly into the skills and rhythms of daily productive life. Aionic time is practiced in many other ways—typically in collective ritual—but school carves out a new space in the culture, a space for the acquisition of new technologies that interrupt, then transform the existing culture. It replaces local knowledge with abstract and universal knowledge, other ways of talking and thinking and understanding ourselves, including new forms of productive time.

Schole is, as *aion* or childhood, a further emergence, a radicalization of school as an experimental zone of subjectivity and of collectivity. The source of this radicalization is philosophy, to the extent that the philosophical impulse turns us inward upon ourselves in the interest, not of techniques for the enhancement of productive time, but of an emergent *new brain*: in the interest of new values, new sensibilities, new capacities, new connections, new centers of meaning, new *bodies*. Thus, there is a struggle between school as a more efficient, far-reaching vehicle for the technical transformation of the chore curriculum, and *schole* as utopia, in the sense of utopia as, after Marcuse (1969: 4) something that "is blocked from coming about by the power of established societies". In school *tout court* [simply], chronos becomes even more intensified because adults impose it on children in this potentially aionic space. In *schole*, as Blake says (1966: 151), "Eternity [aion] is in love with the productions of time." Here we learn to resist the corrosive dichotomies of play/work, fact/value, self/other, and to live in a virtual space of becoming. Are school and *schole* perennially in struggle? Perhaps they are in dialectical tension; time, after all, is one, whatever its modalities. So perhaps we could say that in school, *schole* is a remainder, and visa versa. But today we are in a global situation—the situation of late capitalism and late empire—in which school turns upon and ruthlessly suppresses *schole*, which distorts their relation almost beyond recognition. How are we to deal with this moment of historical excess— when the philosophical impulse is scorned as weakness of nerve, and the deep play of *schole* considered narcissistic and even self-destructive by "the power of established societies"?

WOK: Your questions are increasingly complex and difficult to answer. I am tempted to write that as this last one is so good and powerful we might leave it as it is, without answer and try to move to another. In fact, this kind of writing dialogue is different from an oral one, in that here a reader might suspect that we are in fact answering each other's questions, which I think is not the case. I mean, we are giving a kind of answer, but I would not like them to be taken as ways of closing the questions or as something stable or firm. In relation to this, I would like to add a couple of comments: the first one is that I am now remembering Plato's critique of writing in the *Phaedrus* (274c ff.) and feel quite apprehensive because, in a sense, our written dialogue will not be able to react to the readers' questions. But we do not need to be so Platonic and rely on the power of writing itself. The second has to do with the relationship between questions and answers. In philosophy, questions prevail over answers. I do not mean that only questions count or that answers do not count at all, but that in this exercise of questioning and answering, questions seems to have a privileged position, they are at the beginning and at the end, they open and close thinking and dialogue; they resist all sort of answers; they renew themselves in new questions; so that whatever answers we are giving to our questions, an interesting way of reading this dialogue might be through its questions, even those that eventually appear in our answers. In any case, let me write something about your question; but before doing this, just another short remark: the kinds of questions beginning with "how..." and "how are we to deal with..." are specially difficult because they are asking for some sort of way, path, method or whatever that supports a given direction, and these kinds of issues seem to me less interesting to try to transfer from one person to another. I mean that the answer to this kind of question is even more difficult than any other and in a sense meaningless, in that nobody can answer it for anyone but themself.

At this point I can imagine a reader's anxiousness with my delay in answering your question, and now I am going to get to it. There is a tendency to consider our time a terrible time, one of the most terrible ones in human history. It might be, but I am not so sure. I am not defending it, but probably the place of philosophy as critical questioning has never been much more comfortable or strong, and the forces against *schole*, although different in nature, have never been weaker. We live in times where utopia seems to be losing force and the big words have been badly treated or captured by the forces of the market. Philosophy itself, in its most official aspect, has been reduced to a kind of sophisticated game, less worried about the problems of the life than ever; but at the same time we are seeing new forms of philosophical practice, reconnecting philosophy to life and the outside world. To what extent do these practices share an approach to philosophy as a form of an examined life with other lives? To what extent do they really challenge and put into question the dogmatic forces of the present, or do they simply reinforce them? In other words, to what extent is the practice of philosophy a recreation of *schole* or a fiction that plays the games of the dominant forces? Maybe we can go back to childhood, the main issue of our dialogue: how do you think childhood enters this game?

DK: I love your celebration of the question—it is what for me is most deeply satisfying in the practice of philosophical dialogue, although many, it seems, find the persistence of questions irritating, and a waste of productive time. But I do not agree that the "how" questions are purely personal and meaningless. I have long observed that communal philosophical inquiry, as it works its way into a question, tends to converge on its ethical implications, which in turn converge on Kant's (1993/1785) and Tolstoy's (2012) question, which is the same question put to John the Baptist in the New Testament (Holy Bible, Luke 3: 10–15, 1977: 600): "What then must we do?" John told his questioners tersely to share their goods, not to cheat, and not to abuse power—in short, matters of *dikaiosyne* and *dikaion*.

I notice that Kant says "What must **I** do?" rather than "**we** do", but I would like to emphasize the latter, because I assume we are both understanding *schole* as a "we" situation—a collective—and therefore an ethical situation, because it is about life with others. *Schole* is also by definition a *philosophical* "we" situation in that philosophy is, as you say, "an experience of thinking in *aion*", and *aion* is the distinguishing mark of *schole*. Philosophy as aionic thinking undergoes what you call "the lived experience of putting one's own life into question", and that is an ethical experience. Ethical experience, I have suggested, invokes action ("What must we *do*?"). This, for me, is the link between *schole* and the world of productive time. In that philosophy tends to seek the ethical normative like water seeks its own level, philosophy's chief product is *dikaiosyne*. I would suggest that the school that has been transformed by *schole* provides a working bridge between the two kinds of time—*aion* and *chronos*—a space where the creative tension between the two suggests new styles of productive time outside the school walls.

Maybe I can find my way back to childhood through the difficulty you point out in judging the nature of our times. It seems to me that the worse it gets, the more visible is what it could or should or might be. For example, what Zizek (2011) calls the "second nature" of the "totally '*mediatized*' subject, fully immersed in virtual reality", who while "'spontaneously' he thinks that he is in direct contact with reality is in fact sustained by complex digital machinery" (314) as in *The Matrix* (1999)—is for childhood simply an opportunity for transcending that form of subjectivity through play—or, as Heraclitus says, "childing" (*paizon*). So in *The Matrix* the child in the Oracle's waiting room bends the spoon telekinetically and tells Neo, "there is no spoon… It is not the spoon that bends, it is only yourself." Here "child childing" is seen as the open space of possibility in human evolution. And for this very reason, the death of a child in war is the most heinous instance of the crime against humanity that war is, because that child represents the concrete possibility of a world without war. The child embodies the moral question put to the times, and thus the conscience of the times. So, if philosophy's role in *schole* is an active one, even an activ*ist* one—one that, as you say, models "new forms of philosophical practice, reconnecting philosophy to life and the outside world" and dares "challenge and put into question the dogmatic forces of the present"—what is the role of the child in producing *dikaiosyne* in school as *schole*? Can children be political actors in the world of productive time—can they take to the streets and denounce the oppressors, the greedy and the warmongers? Or should we be satisfied with school/*schole* as Dewey's "embryonic community life", a sort of think tank for the future of human subjectivity and collective identity, as in today's democratic schools movement (http://en.wikipedia.org/wiki/Democratic_education)? Or—as I strongly suspect you might argue—should we carry no expectations at all?

WOK: I also do not think that the "how questions" are personal or meaningless (if they are, they are so just in a very specific aspect), but simply that it is impossible or inconvenient that someone could respond to them for another. And I do agree that philosophy as the practice of *schole* is committed to the ethical and political which means with the other, the "we". In Spanish this is shown by the word for we, "nos-otros", "we-others". What kind of commitment we are referring to is more difficult to be precise. It seems that it is open to a variety of possibilities. I think we can always expect the unexpectable or, as Heraclitus puts it in Fragment 18, we should expect it if we do not want to leave it with no path or way. I mean, we do not know. We never know. This is the only real philosophical knowledge, and even though the world seems in one of its most closed moments, yes, there are new beings at every moment coming into the world, and human history is never ended. This is also the strength of *chronos*. And of *aion* and *schole*: there we act as if the impossible was necessary—"as if", as Kant would say.

We really do not know. Children are political actors just as we are, and what concerns me more is what we can do, through the practice of philosophy as *schole*, to give them the conditions or the space to live the political life, which is a "we" life—that is, which includes the other; which feels and thinks it is worthwhile to live, and which is ready to accept other forms of collective life than the ones we ourselves would expect to live. Of course in a sense we are part of that political life, at least in the conditions we are offering our children in which to build it, so we should not be afraid about it, but we should care about the political forces involved, and the limits of those conditions. How do we think through these political conditions? How do we practice them? Are they really so different from the oppressive world we so much criticize? In what way is the philosophical life preferable to the political life? Or to put it in other words, why are the politics of philosophy worth any more than the politics of the political order? Maybe children can help us to think about these questions. Maybe they can help us to change our questions. Maybe they will come up with new questions. Maybe they can help us to think what we have not thought, or even the unthinkable. Maybe they can educate us. This is what *philosophy for children* is about: not the education of childhood but a child-like education, a philosophical education through the voices of childhood.

Bibliography

Blake, W. (1966) 'The Marriage of Heaven and Hell', in Geoffrey Keynes (ed.), *Blake: The Complete Writings*. Oxford: Oxford University Press, pp. 148–60.

Foucault, M. (1994/1978) 'Entretien avec Michel Foucault'. Entretien avec D. Trombadori, in Dits et Écrits. Paris: Gallimard, vol. IV, pp. 41–95.

Frye, N. (1947) *Fearful Symmetry : A Study of William Blake*. Princeton: Princeton University Press.

Heraclitus (2001) *Heraclitus* (ed. Miroslav Marcovich). Sankt Augustin: Academia Verlag.

Kant, I. (1993/1785) *Grounding for the Metaphysics of Morals* (3rd ed.). Trans. James W. Ellington. Indianapolis: Hackett.

King James Bible (1977) *Holy Bible in the King James Version*. Nashville: Thomas Nelson.

Lancy, D. (2008) *The Anthropology of Childhood: Cherubs, Chattels, Changelings*. Cambridge: Cambridge University Press.

Liddell, H. and Scott, R. (1966) *A Greek English Lexicon*. Oxford: Clarendon Press.

Lyotard, J.-F. (1988) *Le Postmoderne expliqué aux enfants*. Paris: Gallimard.

Marcuse, H. (1969). *An Essay on Liberation*. Boston: Beacon Press.

Plato (1990) *Platonis Opera* (ed. John Burnet). Oxford: Oxford University Press. Trad. Eng. *The Dialogues of Plato*. Trans. B. Jowett (1989). New York: Oxford University Press.

Rancière, J. (1988) 'Ecole, production, égalité', in Xavier Renou (ed.). *L'école de la démocratie*. Paris: Edilig, Fondation Diderot.

Spinoza, B. (1996) *Ethics*. Trans. Edwin Curley. London: Penguin Books.

The Matrix (1999). Directors: The Wachowski Brothers. Distributor: Warner Brothers.

Tolstoy, L. (2012) *What Shall We Do?* London: The Free Age Press.

Winnicott, D. W. (1971) *Playing and Reality*. New York: Basic Books.

Zizek, S. (2011) *Living in the End Times*. London: Verso.

Part I

Inspiration for a childlike education

1 Teaching as verification of equality

Jacques Rancière and *The Ignorant Schoolmaster*

The Brazilian reception

To begin with, I would like to position the reception of Jacques Rancière's *The Ignorant Schoolmaster* in the context of Brazil, where I've been working for the last few years. In this country, the field of philosophy of education is a very complex one. There is a very strong influence of Christian thinking when it comes to the theoretical approach found in teacher formation, many of them coming from religious seminars. A second important point of reference is the influence of Marxism and, more often than expected, a combination of these two tendencies, under the motto of what could be called a "critical-progressive" education. In effect, a sort of Christian-Marxism, faithful, and devoted, positions itself, theoretically, to overcome inequalities and social injustices through a critical work in the educational institutions: we teach to transform society, to build a critical conscience that will bring revolutionary changes to a society—such as the Brazilian one—that has been waiting for such changes for centuries.

On the fringes of this dominant tendency—with many aspects and versions, more or less Marxist, more or less Christian, simplified to the extreme here—there is a dissemination of small groups working with philosophy of education, in dialogue with different contemporary philosophical orientations: transcendental pragmatism, psychoanalysis, hermeneutic, phenomenology, neo-pragmatism, post-structuralism, critical theory, etc. A matter that concerns many philosophers of education of diverse trends is the teaching of philosophy in many different levels. In Brazil, philosophy is now a mandatory discipline in high school, one that is increasing and expanding[1].

These proclivities that we mentioned before began to inscribe themselves institutionally in the formation of the educators who in many cases come from seminaries, teaching programs or social sciences. If in the former cases the teaching of Philosophy of Education is strong but distinctly doctrinal, in the latter it is almost non-existent. In this sense, many educators do what they can: carry out an introduction to the main field and topics of classic philosophy, a manualized history of the philosophical ideas about education, an overview of the major schools of thought that exist in Brazilian education; in other words, they carry out a synthetic presentation and application of philosophical current ideas into the field of education.

Within this context, it is not hard to imagine the doubts and mistrust surrounding the acceptance of a thought such as J. Rancière's, specifically toward his book *The Ignorant Schoolmaster,* a text in which the philosophical intervention focuses on an educational situation. The Portuguese translation of Rancière's book was published in Brazil in 2002. This edition has specially written preface (though unpublished) in which Rancière refers to *The Ignorant Schoolmaster* and its relevance to the Brazilian context. In that same year, Rancière presented the book in the First French-Brazilian Colloquium of Philosophy of Education at the State University of Rio de Janeiro. In 2003, the prestigious magazine *Educação & Sociedade* (Campinas, 24, 82, 2003) published a Dossier titled "Freedom and Equality in Education. With regards of *The Ignorant Schoolmaster*",[2] featuring an interview with J. Rancière by Patrice Vermeren, Laurence Cornu, and Andrea Benvenuto and texts from a dozen professors from different countries that establish a dialogue with Rancière's book.

The context of the instituted policy marked the upswing of progressivism in Brazil at this time with Lula and the Workers' Party's victory in the 2002 presidential elections. Education was in the air, acting as the engine and driving force of the social transformations that the country had been asking for since its colonial times. Within this frame of exuberant optimism, *The Ignorant Schoolmaster* is an ungodly appearance that questions and threatens the foundations of such optimism. Therefore, this book has been received with some enthusiasm in Brazil; but above all, it is also a source of uneasiness for many people.

Part of the discomfort has to do with the style of the book. In an academia that focuses on apparently more solid discourses and serious treatises and manuals, one in which the explanation, so criticized by Jacotot, is the key of the pedagogical mechanism, such an unpretentious and systematic story is somewhat doomed to be underestimated as a fable, as pure fiction. The obsession with explaining pedagogical pretenses, trends and movements is at odds with a story that not only does not offer explicative outlines, but also leaves us without methods for teaching, learning or explaining (even though it does not do without its own explanations).

There are also philosophical issues, political and untimely controversies that go against the dominant way of thinking in the educational field. I will mention only a few of them: Perception of Humanity, Tautology of Potentiality, the Relationship between Will and Intelligence, the Uniqueness of Intelligence, Equality as a Principle, the Relationship between Ignorance and Inequality, Criticism to Explanation and Transmission, the Absence of a Method...

Despite all that, the most controversial matters that arise from *The Ignorant Schoolmaster* are, above all, political. In the aforementioned interview, Rancière clarifies some ideas that look similar to the most influential thinker of Brazilian Modern Education: Paulo Freire. Rancière situates Freire along with Jacotot;

they are faced with the positivist and pedagogical slogan of "Order and Progress" where both disrupt the assumed harmony between social order and intellectual order. However, Rancière also makes sure he lays out the difference between them: nothing is more divergent from Jacotot than a method for social "consciousness". In contrast with the most influential Latin American pedagogue of our time, Jacotot attests that equality is strictly an individual matter and that it is impossible for it to be institutionalized.

It is here where Rancière leaves room for one possible approach: although intellectual emancipation fails to flourish within the social context, there is not a social emancipation that does not presuppose an individual one. In this sense, as Rancière himself suggests in the interview, something links Jacotot's anarchism to Paulo Freire's optimism: "In the process for intellectual emancipation as a vector of movements of political emancipation that breaks social logic, a logic of institution" (*Educação & Sociedade,* 2003: 199).

With all that, we argue that the distances between Jacotot-Rancière and Paulo Freire are fundamental and are exponents of the principles and ways of understanding politics. According to Rancière, politics, derived from an axiom of equality, is an exceptional phenomenon in history. In contrast, for Freire, education is just a political act of emancipation per excellence. If for Rancière the figure of the teacher and the emancipator are never to be confused with one another, thus following different logics ("Being an emancipator is always possible as long as the role of an intellectual emancipator it is not to be confused with the role of a teacher (…) it is necessary to distantiate the reasons (…) an emancipator is not a teacher (…) It is possible to be a teacher, a citizen, and emancipator; but it is not possible to be all three under only one logic", *Educação & Sociedade,* 2003: 201), for Freire, on the contrary, those roles are not dissociable: a teacher who does not emancipate is a teacher who does not deserve to be called a teacher; being a teacher only makes sense (politically) when the pedagogical relationship is turned into a drive for emancipation, understood as an act of love, dialogue, and the consciousness-raising of the oppressed. In this sense, in a context where the optimism of Freire is profoundly influential, a death blow to any easy optimism will generate quick defenses and antibodies.

At last, there is another aspect in the political criticism of *The Ignorant Schoolmaster,* perhaps a more interesting as well as defiant one. It is said that the book could carry out an appropriate critical function in a European country such as France, with a modern and consolidated State, with a public school system that even with its problems still has the appropriate level of a developed country when it comes to the index of universality, illiteracy, school dropout and grade retention—incomparably superior to the ratings of Brazil. In contrast, in a country that has not been able to include all its population into the school institution, with an educational public system weakened and destabilized by the latest privatizing and elitist educational reforms, with schools on the verge of collapse, it is argued from the dominant pedagogical establishment that a decentralizing criticism such as the one of *The Ignorant Schoolmaster* could only have a conservative and regressive effect: it weakens what is public, precisely what needs to be strengthened in the face of the present pretension of the hegemony of the market and the private sector.

Even though the country has made significant progress during the last decade in terms of school inclusion, the context of established politics in Brazil after a period of more than ten years of the Workers' Party government generates less and less political optimism; the general lines in relation to the reception of *The Ignorant Schoolmaster* have not changed. With this essay, we are not proposing a defense of this book. On the one hand, we have done that in the presence of its critics[3]; on the other hand, it seems more interesting to think from these lines of inquiry about some problems situated between philosophy, politics, and education.

A politic of disagreement?

We believe that part of the nuisance that *The Ignorant Schoolmaster* provokes in this context allows space for the visibility of one of its main virtues: a revitalizing way of understanding and reaffirming philosophy in the educational field. As in the Presentation of this book, it is worth recalling the distinction that M. Foucault made between two different types of books, or better yet, between two types of relationships that we establish with writing: a relation of truth or a relation based on experience. In the case of the former, a book functions as something that is written to pass along what we know or that it is read to learn what is unknown; to communicate thoughts or to learn what others are thinking about. The latter, in turn, is a book that functions as a device that allows us to question the truths in which the author or the reader is embedded. If in the first instance the relation legitimates a truth, then the second one problematizes that truth and the relationship with it. If a relationship of truth leaves the author and his thoughts intact, the writing and reading as experience transform oneself and others.

A book so beautifully written such as *The Ignorant Schoolmaster* invites us to enter a relation based on experience, to settle in a destabilizing and critical way of thinking. Conversely, if we read *The Ignorant Schoolmaster* as a book of truths, we would not profit from it; moreover, it would actually be put to death, which is something that the book seems to fight from beginning to end. On the contrary, as a reading experience, Jacotot and Rancière can help us to think differently about the matters in question. In the case of the readers/teachers, the experience of the teacher Jacotot can help us to be teachers in a different way.

In order to get the most out of Jacotot, we have to sit with him shoulder to shoulder, as equals—this expression has never been more on point; we must allow him to make us feel uncomfortable, to provoke us, to make us fret. In this sense, there is an undeniable philosophical and political value of a way of thinking that does not leave things the same way it found them: quite the opposite, it will trap the reader in a circle from which he or she will have to make their own way out, and with a quite different perspective to the one he or she entered with.

It is here where the interesting and problematic part starts, because it is noticeable that a reading experience that puts out and makes people fret will demand new places and new relationships. And in this sense, *The Ignorant Schoolmaster* remains silent. It does not prescribe or authorize. There is an emptiness, and absence; there are neither methods nor paths. Up to here, there is no problem. Quite the opposite, pedagogy is so filled with easy, simplifying and superficial answers, that a little bit of silence will help it breathe! One can see there the proper gesture of philosophy, one with a unique elegance. There is nothing more interesting for a teaching or learning situation than the emptiness which creates space to think about the "how", "where", "when", or "what" of education. The point of the matter is that in *The Ignorant Schoolmaster* there is not only absence of prescription but also that the last word appears to be the impossibility, a normalized negation: "No political party, government, army, school nor institution will ever emancipate a single person" (Rancière, 2004: 132).

In other words, *The Ignorant Schoolmaster* plays with the value and the context of an educational practice between equality and emancipation. The relationship is circular: it departs from one concept to arrive at the other one. At the same time, it verifies the former one. The problem is that both of them can never encounter each other in a formal social context: "Universal teaching is not and cannot be a social method; it cannot be extended on or by the social institutions" (ibid.: 135); the alternative is exclusive: "it is necessary to choose between creating an unequal society with equal men, or an equal society with unequal men" (ibid.: 171). Emancipation does not go beyond a relationship between individuals: there is not and there cannot be in *The Ignorant Schoolmaster* an emancipating and educational project.

Thus, the philosophical gesture prompts a political and chimerical disagreement (there is only politics in dreams: "to dream an emancipated society that would be a society of artists", ibid.: 95); it also prompts a distance, an excision, and an impossibility ("a man can be reasonable, not a citizen", ibid.: 112), there is no margin ("a citizen knows the reason of the civic madness. But, at the same time, he knows it as insurmountable", ibid.: 117).

According to Rancière-Jacotot, this absence of political possibilities, at least in the states where there is social normalcy in institutions and schools, should take them into conformity: "it would be sufficient to learn to be men of equal status in an unequal society. This is what emancipation means" (ibid.: 171); "Without a doubt, emancipated people are respectful towards social order. They know that social order is, at any rate, better than disorder" (ibid: 136). It is true that the emancipated ones do not give in to social order ("But it is all he can be given, and no institution could be satisfied at this minimum", ibid.) but they neither threaten social order ("He knows what he can expect of a social order and he would not provoke big disruptions", ibid.: 141).

We are interested in discussing those implications that have a certain air of pessimism or fatalism within *The Ignorant Schoolmaster*. Ultimately, it is about questioning opinions with other opinions. Opinions of resistance against other opinions of resistance.

Let it be clear: we are not interested in affirming simple optimism. Perhaps it could be interesting to think about different ways of optimism. There are simple optimisms: to believe that everything is wonderful, possible or that things will turn for the better, more or less at a fast pace. We do not share this type of optimism, but only the one that attests for the idea that things can always be different, a Foucauldian type of optimism ("My optimism consists rather in saying: there are so many things that can be changed, as fragile as they are, more related to contingencies than to needs, more to arbitrariness rather than to evidence, more complex and temporary historical contingencies as opposed to inevitable anthropological constant" (Foucault, 1994/1981: 182)). History is not closed; the last word has never been said. Ultimately, it is also about a Jacototist motive: "The 'I cannot' it is not a name of any fact" (Rancière, 2004: 76); "It is about confirming the power of reason, to observe what it can be done with it, or what reason can do to maintain itself active at the center of extreme madness" (ibid.: 124). To be optimistic does not necessarily mean to be a naive progressist.

We live at the center of extreme civic madness; perhaps more clearly in Latin America where inequality reigns. It is true that in some of our countries—Bolivia, Ecuador, maybe they are the best examples—there are interesting political experiences now being carried out. But in the general scheme of things there is little space for politics, there is no serious democracy, there is only capital and market; in other words, barbarism and exclusion. There are not enough reasons for a progressive optimism: nothing to make us think that something radically different could come out from the dominant practice of politics, political parties, and elections of the established institutions. Neither of the pedagogical institutions, such is the case and the desolation of public education. However, there is nothing that authorizes us to think that we cannot create a new politics, another type of politics, still with equality as a principle and not as a goal, in the middle of so much madness.

In *The Ignorant Schoolmaster* and in other texts that refer to him, Rancière seems to suggest that it cannot be done. His argument is more or less the following: a) there is only democratic politics; b) democracy is the government of the incompetents (to govern), the breach of the logic of inequality; c) there is no law, chance, consistency, mediation between emancipation of an individual and politics; of the latter, Rancière seems to deduce that d) there is no emancipatory politics, there cannot be politics (democracy, equality) or at least it is an exception, it happens exceptionally (ibid.: 201–2)[4].

The problem, in part, relies on the meaning and context of politics. Rancière characterizes it as: antagonistic to the police (government); paradoxical action; of complementary subjects, derived from a specific rationality;

of rupture against the *arche*, "normal" exercise of power and its dispositions; outlined with an evanescent difference in the distribution of social parts; manifestation of dissension (the presence of two worlds in one). The dominant politics is, therefore, that which utilizes the mask of democracy, represents the police, the strongest negation of a politics with equality as a principle (1997; 2004).

Are we facing an exception of politics? Does politics exist nowadays? We believe that it does exist—in Latin America, for example, in the Zapatistas' politics. It is true that it is an exception, but it is not an *iure* exception. Whether there is or not politics, it is not a matter of *iure* but rather of experience: and the challenge is to think and affirm the conditions where politics can be experienced.

To sentence the *iure* impossibility of politics seems to contribute to the establishment of the police: it looks functional to the dominant inequality and aggressive to philosophical thinking. It is about establishing another type of politics, first in the way of thinking, a politics of constant inquiry about the possibility and the ways of politics itself, to unsettle impossibility. An open politics of disconformity and dissatisfaction that, departing from equality and without knowing the origin of itself, gets impatient with the dominant civic madness and looks for a way to disrupt it.

Pedagogy and education

Perhaps the pessimistic tone that seems predominant in *The Ignorant Schoolmaster* and in other surrounding texts has to do with the fact that it is a philosophical exercise of thinking about a pedagogical situation. Jacotot and Rancière know well the temptations of pedagogy: "Every pedagogy is spontaneously progressive" (Rancière, 2004: 153) and also about its risks: "Progress is a pedagogical fiction built upon fiction of the whole society" (ibid.). Perhaps, for Rancière, the absence of politics in education is clearer than in other fields; there he can find the logic of inequality in its most natural and naturalized habitat.

Thereupon, the spirit of Jacotot reappears with all its might: the ignorant ones rebel. The circle breaks again. At last, it can begin from anywhere. And what happens once could happen again thousands of times. Potentiality of emancipation. We have to follow intelligence. We have to search. We always have to search.

We think of differentiating pedagogy and education, a distinction akin to the one between politics and police. Pedagogy is the government of the ones that "know", the organization, structuration and legitimation of knowledge and the methods of communicating them, the realm of the explanatory logic in the pedagogical institutions. On the contrary, education is the government of those who "do not know", incompetents, unskillful.

Pedagogy denies the initial equality and the final emancipation that education presupposes and makes possible: While the former affirms hierarchies everywhere, the latter is only possible when there are no hierarchies. If pedagogy is the realm of the discipline of bodies, knowledge and thoughts, then education is its indiscipline, particularly the indiscipline of thoughts, so that one does not think of what one is supposed to, but rather of the things order and discipline would not allow us to think of otherwise.

There is, exceptionally, education when the logic of pedagogy is interrupted; when truths leave space for experience in the pedagogical institutions. Nothing in thinking can deny the rights to the possibility of education. Quite the opposite, we ask ourselves incessantly about the conditions that make education possible.

We share the reading experience of *The Ignorant Schoolmaster* in courses of philosophy of education with teachers and soon-to-be teachers of the most diverse social classes. We have gone out to divulge the news within our own. We enjoy the disruptive and dismissive power. We invite people to create ways of verifying equality. We smile when we see the happiness of those that do not accept the logic of superiors and inferiors. At last, just how Jacotot had taught us, universal education is the method of the poor (ibid.: 137).

All in all, inspired by the inscription of Père Lachaise, we open the end of the story. We disrupt the Jacototist circular ending: to emancipate oneself has nothing to do with being a conformist; the same way ignorance, it is of any presupposed impossibility. We ask questions about some of the answers: what is the place of philosophy between pedagogy and education? What are the conditions that we need in order to have education, that is to say, politics and emancipation in the context of teaching and learning? How can we propitiate, from an equalitarian logic, practices that will break the logic of the prevailing inequality in the pedagogical institutions? And lastly, why do we teach (what we teach) and we learn (what we learn) pierced through, the way we are, by pedagogy and the police? The interesting part of finalizing with questions is the suggestion that there is more thinking to do, above all, in the middle of so much madness.

Notes

1 For a more detailed account of the situation of the teaching of philosophy of education in Brasil, cf Fávero, Altair Alberto, Ceppas, Filipe, Gontijo, Pedro Ergnaldo, Gallo, Sílvio and Kohan, Walter. 'O ensino da filosofia no Brasil: um mapa das condições atuais'. *Cad. CEDES*, Campinas, SP, vol. 24, n. 64, dic. 2004, pp. 257–84.

2 This Dossier, with some modifications, was published later in Journals of Colombia, Argentina, Spain and France: *Educación y Pedagogía* (Universidad de Antioquía, Colombia, v. xv, n. 36, 2003, pp. 1–155, *Cuaderno de Pedagogía* (Universidad Nacional de Rosario, Argentina, n. 11, 2003), *Diálogos* (Valencia, España, n. 36, 2003) and *Le Télémaque* (Presses Universitaires de l'Université de Caen, v. 27, May 2005).

3 To this effect we dedicate chapter 6 ("Una infancia del enseñar y del aprender") of our book *Infancia. Entre educación y filosofía* (Cf. Kohan, 2004).

4 In Rancière himself this is a polemic issue. In other texts, he seems more open and positive: "the matter, in that case, is not simply to confront a 'political problem'. It is to reinvent politics" (2004).

Bibliography

Educação & Sociedade (2003) Dossier: 'Igualdade e liberdade em educação. A propósito de *O mestre ignorante*.' Jorge Larrosa and Walter Kohan, v. 24, n. 82.

Foucault, M. (1994/1981) "Est-il donc important de penser?" Entretien avec Didier Eribon. *Libération*, n. 15, 30–31 mai 1981, p. 21. In *Dits et Écrits*. Paris: Gallimard, 1994/1981, vol. IV, pp. 178–82.

Freire, P. (1996) *Pedagogia da autonomia*. São Paulo: Paz e Terra.

———. (2005) *Pedagogia do Oprimido*. São Paulo: Paz e Terra.

Kohan, W. (2004) *Infancia. Entre educación y filosofia*. Barcelona: Laertes.

Rancière, J. (1987) *Le maître ignorant*. Paris: Fayard.

———. (1997) 'Onze thèses sur la politique', *Filozofski Vestnik*. Ljiublijana, v. XVIII, n. 2.

———. (2004) 'Política, identificación, subjetivación', *Metapolítica*. México, n. 36, julio/agosto.

2 The teaching of the courage of living in Socrates and the Cynics

Michel Foucault

Michel Foucault and philosophy

Philosophy escapes all ambitions of entrapment, even the ones that emerge within itself. As a concept and as an institution, it resists all pretensions of confinement of its totalization or universalization. Philosophy and its practice, its historical movement, its untimely progression or what is done in its name cannot be enclosed in one place only.

There is between us, a dominant, established, and institutionalized form within that pretension: one that affirms itself with an exegesis of philosophical doctrines of a textual corpus constituted by the philosophers of the so-called "Occidental tradition". It would have its birth in Ancient Greece—curiously, from someone who does not write any type of texts or doctrines, like Socrates, whom, for those that want to move back the birth a bit further, mark, too, the moment: the "pre-Socratics", the "ones before Socrates". This tradition would be followed by us and be activated now, mainly, in the Philosophy Departments of the most prestigious universities of Europe and the United States, the legitimate followers of such noble tradition.

Such history has its own and most established names as well as the damned names; the renowned and the forgotten ones, the acclaimed and repudiated ones. It is accompanied by powerful institutional devices that allow it to circulate and expand: resources for investigation, libraries, conferences, editorials, courses of different levels and other tools. It is good to perceive that, regardless of its sophisticated and impenetrable appearance, such institutionalized philosophy is "barely" an arbitrary and contingent mechanism, with a history that can be studied, understood, and transformed.

Michel Foucault occupies a very singular place in this mechanism. He is an intellectual figure recognized in France, so much so that he occupied a prestigious professorship at *Collège de France* until his death in 1984. Although his relationship with philosophy has always been in question—first, because he himself rejects classifications and pigeonholing—his is an important name if we pay attention to some of the most evident indicators. He is one of those responsible for establishing the University of Vincennes (nowadays Paris VIII), to the rhythm of the occurrences of May '68, and he is an acclaimed figure in the events of the field, a guaranteed editorial event, a name that, despite the resistances in the most enclosed and dogmatic academic philosophical circles, is hardly questioned as an important reference in contemporary philosophy, even if it is to criticize him or to condemn him.

To ratify these tensions a little, Foucault shows himself in his texts and in his life to be a bit uncomfortable in that narrative. His way of applying a philosophical thought, his militancy, collides with the most regular practices in academic philosophy. His field of dialogue and thought is always greater than a strict circle, always touching upon problems of the "present time" and of "the social life" that philosophers are accustomed to consider distant from their academic concerns. He is more concerned with the problems of human beings than the problems of professional philosophers. Furthermore, his books are not very orthodox; he rarely writes about other philosophers, his works are not about philosophical concepts in the classical context; his audience of scholars and readers widely exceeds the usual in this discipline.

The last part of his pedagogical life is the clearest testimony of this tension. In fact, it is common to differentiate three stages in Michel Foucault's philosophical thought: One geared towards issues about language (that some relate to "archeology"); another one that is focused on the notion of power (called "genealogy"), and finally, a stage that is focused on the issue of subject (denominated "ethics"). Although this distinction could have a heuristic value, we could consider it insufficient and problematic inasmuch as it presupposes exactly what Foucault tried to revitalize throughout his whole life and, predominantly, in the last courses taught at the *Collège de France*: a conception of philosophy as the history of philosophical doctrines, of which Foucault himself would become part of, with the aspects given by relevant topics addressed in each stage of his thought. That reading, many times concerned in defense of the philosophical beliefs originated from academia, would be paradoxically legitimating a conception of philosophy affirmed by it, inscribing Foucault in that same tradition that he himself does not perceive so affirmatively.

According with the hypothesis that we want to contend for in this present chapter—which is barely a hypothesis of reading and thinking—Foucault, on the contrary, could not be located in outlines of this type under penalty of deadly wounding the conception that he has about philosophy, his main interest, his *leitmotiv*, his own way of experimenting and practicing philosophy. In other words, the hypothesis that we defend here is that Foucault attests to a conception of philosophy that turns out to be inconvenient or even meaningless to study and chronologize his thoughts in the way presented before; that is, starting from the topics and the main interests in many moments of his work.

We present this hypothesis and we defend it with testimonies from Foucault's last course, his final legacy. To say this once and clearly: Foucault conceives philosophy as a form of life, and the philosophy in which he could and would like to include himself is not the philosophy that dominates academia, but a philosophy that is active, a live exercise to problematize the meaning of a philosophical life. It is within this context that he searches in ancient times for traces of a history different from the philosophy that arises from what he denominates a "Cartesian moment" that ends up diverting: not a history of the philosophers' doctrines, but a history of philosophical lives, a history in which a philosophizing life is able to feel at ease with itself. It is for these reasons that, in this narrative, Socrates and the Cynics perform a main role, because if the former is the one who chooses to rather lose his life than to give up telling the truth, the latter ones are those for whom life itself bears witness to truth in a scandalous way.

It is in one of those philosophy histories, still to be traced, that Michel Foucault would like to introduce himself. A history that problematizes the relationships between life and truth of those that called themselves philosophers, a history that problematizes, in each space and in each time, the meaning of living a philosophical life.

Socrates' philosophical life

Michel Foucault's last three courses, *The Hermeneutics of the Subject* (given in 1981–82 and published in French in 2001), *The Government of Self and Others* (given in 1982 and published in 2008), and *The Courage of Truth* (given in 1982 and published in 2009, and which has *The Government of Self and Others II* as a subtitle) all make up a unit given by the notion of *parrhesia*. It is a journey through Greco-Roman culture that begins in 1981 with the course *Subjectivity and Truth,* and whose purpose is to reconsider what we understand as philosophy and its history, at the same time that it departs from a criticism to the traditional way of making history of Greek philosophy and reaches what is understood as philosophy in relation to that same history.

In these courses, Foucault analyzes the problematic field of the relationships between the ways of telling the truth (knowledge), techniques of government (relationships of power), and practices of the self (constitution of the subject) (2009: 10). It is within this frame that Foucault places the specific problem that is crucial to him in his last few years: a truth of life itself, the meaning of a philosophical life, and how his own life can relate with certain ways of living philosophy.

If in *The Government of Self and Others* Foucault demarcates the lines for a history of the "political dramatic of *parrhesia*", in *The Courage of Truth* he proposes the alignments of "philosophical dramatic of *parrhesia*": a *parrhesia* in the philosophical lives of Socrates and the Cynics, something already sketched in the last lessons of *The Government of Self and Others I.*

In Foucault's exposition, Socrates establishes a new form of *parrhesia* (ethical or philosophical), against the traditional ways of telling the truth and the political *parrhesia*. Socrates does not speak at the Assembly—and it is precisely this that adversaries complain about. Instead, he does so at the plazas, streets, gymnasiums, houses around the city and inside the city itself, thus addressing the soul of each individual. Plato's first *dialogues*—also, exactly called Socratic dialogue—clearly show this scene and practice.

In *The Courage of Truth*, Foucault retakes the study of *Alcibiades I*, made in *The Hermeneutic of the Subject*. Also, Foucault was interested in the *Apology of Socrates, Crito and Phaedo*, around the death of Socrates and the *Laches,* that with *Alcibiades I* will be set side by side as two possibilities of understanding the caring of self. As we have studied the reading of the death of Socrates in more detail in another text (cf. Kohan, 2009), here we will present a brief synthesis of the main conclusions of these courses.

Laches exemplifies the three typical moments of the Socratic *parrhesia:* 1) it aims towards investigation (*zetesis*); 2) examination (*exetasis*); 3) care (*epimeleia*). What takes Socrates to the parrhesiastic contract is the search for the meaning of the oracle's affirmation ("There is no one wiser than Socrates in Athens"). In the *Apology*, he offers a justification for this practice; in the *Laches*, Socrates shows himself as a true master of attention, the only one to know how to take care of others so the others can start taking care of themselves.

Also, *Alcibiades I* shows Socrates' *parrhesia* functioning at its best. However, the attention falls over a different object. Socrates shows Alcibiades that his ambitions to govern are completely unfounded. They should be compared to his rivals inside and outside of Athens, the Spartans and the Persians, so it can be perceived that, as is custom in Athens, his education was completely relegated in the hands of a slave. In addition to that, his riches are also lesser, and, to worsen his condition, he lacks a knowledge, an art, *techne,* that could compensate the deficiencies.

Alcibiades accepts, therefore, that he should learn to take care of himself before he can pretend to take care of others. For that, it is necessary to understand that the most important part of himself that needs to be taken care of is the soul and not the body (*Alcibiades I*, 132c). Once this is internalized, it is necessary to understand that taking care of oneself means to know oneself. Finally, that a soul knows itself, in its excellence: wisdom, knowledge, and the thoughts of another soul that reflect what is the best inside of it (*Alcibiades I*, 132d–133c). Thus, in *Alcibiades I*, care is positioned in the knowledge of oneself and, more specifically, in the knowledge of the soul.

In *Laches*, taking care of the self is something different. In a conversation with two eminent politicians of Athens, Laches and Nicias, Socrates teaches a lesson through his *parrhesia*. After establishing the criteria to become an educator, he asks Laches and Nicias to show their credentials, and for that they are required to explain themselves, the lives they have, and why they live the way they do (*Laches*, 187e–188a). Thus, in *Laches,* the way in which one lives—and not the soul—shows whether there is care in a life.

From Foucault's perspective, in these *dialogues* two big lines are born that cross the history of philosophy in the West: the ontology of self (*Alcibiades I*) and the art of existence (*Laches*). The first of those dialogues gives place, already in Plato himself, to the self itself as a reality ontologically separated from the body; the second one to a true discourse that gives shape and style to human existence. The first reading generates a metaphysics; the second, a stylistic or aesthetic of existence (2009: 149).

Socratic *parrhesia* makes of life an "object of elaboration and aesthetic perception": In order to live a life as a beautiful piece of work, we have to work on it in order to shape it. In this, Socrates is not the first—there are precedents as remote as Homer and Pindar—but he produces an inflection: even the ideal of a beautiful life is profoundly ingrained in the Greek tradition, Socrates is the first one to show that a life is necessarily associated with the task of giving account for oneself. In other words, it is not sufficient, unlike what tradition dictates, to live a life and postulate it: it is necessary to be able to justify the beauty of the lived life. Socratic *parrhesia,* just as it is presented in Plato's *dialogues,* is the testimony of his way of justifying a way of living, a lifestyle.

The Foucauldian reading of Socrates has a tone that is strongly celebratory. Foucault appears to be completely seduced by the Athenian. He seems to find in Socrates what he is looking for in his own life. In his reading, the life and death of Socrates are strengthened with the care of oneself, in a beautiful existence and in a true saying. His way of dying is a proof of more caring, it is part of the stylistic of his life. For having established a way of dying as a way of caring, it participates in the stylistic of his life. By founding an ethical and philosophical way of saying the truth, Socrates is irreplaceable as a genealogical moment of a philosophical stylistic. In this way, Foucault seems to find in the Athenian a common stylistic of existence in life and in death: Socrates would mark the beginning of a trajectory of philosophical lives, one in which Foucault wants to see himself.

Life as scandal of truth: the Cynics

Cynicism goes deeper into the relationship that Socrates establishes between truth and life, when he defends himself to the accusers in Plato's *Apology of Socrates,* so much so that Diogenes—and from then on all the Cynics in a general way—was called the "prophet of *parrhesia*" (Foucault, 2009: 156). Some Cynics, just like Socrates, were judged and condemned of irreligiosity. They are men of *parrhesia.* Cynicism is a way of radicalizing Socratism that transposes all the limits that condition the true saying. It is a school of life characterized more by the practice of a style of existence rather than by the development of a very sophisticated theoretical framework. A Cynic way of life has very precise conditions, characteristics and rules, but its doctrinal field is very narrow and limited.

Foucault finds (2009: 154 ff.), in a text of Epictetus (*Conversations III*), a self-reflection about nature and the meaning of the Cynic way of life. The Cynic is compared to a spy (*kataskopos*) of the army, the type of spy who goes to the lines of the enemy to locate what could be favorable or hostile to the army itself, and to anticipate where he could be attacked from and how the enemy would think of launching an attack, in order to be alert and reduce it. The Cynic is a messenger with no attachments to anyone or anything; therefore, he is without a motherland, an errant so that he can approach the others and throw some light on the future. In order to be that messenger and to announce the truth of the future without fear or censorship, his condition must always be in a state of detachment with regards to life, one that is free and self-determined.

For this reason, the Cynic is also a man of walking stick, of bare feet, of poverty, of filth, he becomes detached of everything that could generate conditioning. His life makes him give up all that is useless, that is not essential, meaning everything that is conventional and unnatural, everything that can be done without, not necessary, unsettling the essential nakedness that humanity can attain.

Moreover, because of this, he lives apart from society. In such a way, his life shows the only life worthy of a human being, what should be a life worth living for. He is the radicalization of Socratism: the Cynic lives his own life as a manifestation of truth, as an *alethurgia* (2009: 158–9).

In so doing, Cynicism would be the movement that takes to the extreme a true life (*alethes bios*), from its own precept, of a divine command that Diogenes, like Socrates, receives from the oracle of Delphi as a mission: " 'adulterate the coinage' or 'deface the currency' " (*parakharattein to nomisma*, 2009: 208). From the etymological proximity between *nomisma* (money) and *nomos* (law), Foucault reads in that mission the task of putting into question the order— philosophical and political—in order to transform it.

A Cynic life would be that same life of tradition: a) an unconcealed life, completely visible and public in all its forms, with nothing to hide; on the contrary, everything in that life can be shown entirely; b) a life without mixing nor dependency, lived dramatically under the most absolute way of poverty and scarcity, provoked by the most radical material-detachment; for the Cynics everything is reduced to the minimum to avoid any kind of dependency: clothing, feeding, shelter; c) a straight life according to the precepts of nature and the rejection of every or any social convention. Goodness comes from nature and only from nature; evil comes from human forms that have to be rejected and condemned systematically; therefore, to have a dog's life is not a choice but a duty. In a more general way, animality is a material and moral model of a Cynic existence. Finally, d) a sovereign life, master of oneself and also a life of helping others, a life that procures to make of its own sovereignty a universal lesson, one to be learned by all human beings. The Cynic has a mission and is to transmit that lesson, and to do it in an active and polemic way, biting, attacking.

This is an image of Foucault needed to understand the refutation character of this movement: "cynicism as a mask of the real life" (2009: 209): an extrapolation, a reversion, so characteristic that it is impossible for the dominant philosophy not to accept Cynicism as its own, as part of it. At the same time, it is so opposite of the life lived from that philosophy that the disdain and the desire to expel Cynicism out of the world of philosophy is quite inevitable.

A Cynic life is so sovereign that Diogenes is more of a King than Alexander (2009: 253–5): moreover, Diogenes is the only true king since in order to secure his authority and be able to apply it, Alexander depends on many things (such as the army, allies, armors, etc.). Diogenes, on the contrary, does not depend on anything or anyone. Furthermore, Alexander became a king whereas Diogenes has always been a king, by nature, as the son of Zeus. On the other hand, it does not matter how many times Alexander defeats his external enemies, because he will always have to fight against his internal enemies, his defects and vices that, unlike him, the sage does not have. Finally, Alexander could lose his power any time, while Diogenes will always remain as the king. Thus, Diogenes is the only true king, a king so dedicated as ignored, so miserable as hidden, but with all this, he is nonetheless the only and true king.

In this way, the Cynic is a combatant, a militant, a member of the resistance. He fights against himself, against his desires—he also fights against the laws, customs, and established norms. He is a combatant and his arms, the way he transmits his lesson, they are all punctual, abrupt, and violent actions. He is not an educator or a people's trainer. He shakes them, he turns them through minimal gestures, but profound and radical. He is a sniper of a philosophical life so urgent and needed as impossible to be accepted by other human beings, philosophers included.

Within this scheme of things, Cynicism would be not only a current of classic philosophy but a way of life and denouncement that scandalizes its own philosophical community: life as a scandal of truth. It would be retaken by practices so diverse such as Christian asceticism, revolutionary movements in the mid-nineteenth century, Russian nihilism, European and American anarchism, the revolutionary parties in their emergence in the 1920s, modern art, and carnivalesque practices (2009: 166 ff.).

Following this are the characteristics of a cynical practice (2009: 219–21). The first four are quite traditional, and the fifth one is specifically cynical: a) philosophy is a preparation for life; b) this preparation consists in taking responsibility of oneself, taking care of oneself; c) the only studies needed in this preparation are the ones useful for existence; d) life must be coherent with the precepts that are formulated for it: this is, at last, the specificity of Cynicism; e) that life must "adulterate the coinage", what could be understood superficially or derogatorily, as a falsification task, and more profoundly as a task to break and smash all the habits and norms that are in force to demolish and transform them in the sense of naturalizing and animalizing human life.

When he discusses some interpretations of Cynicism, Foucault fights against (2009: 166) the reading that sees in it an individualist movement. The heart of Cynicism is in life in the form of scandal of the truth, life as a privileged place of manifestation of truth and the militancy for social life, for man as a whole, for the universe of humanity.

Platonism and Cynicism are two forms of Socratism that gave place to two confronted forms of relationship to oneself: first, the cognitive work and the purification of oneself, and particularly, of the soul; and second, the limited practices of life, the answering of life by life itself, or the scandal of a true life.

Philosophy as a philosophical life

We are used to seeing, in the history of philosophy, a set of ideas, doctrines and theoretical positions about certain subjects or problems. And we are also used to reclaiming a place for Foucault no less in that history. It does not seem fortuitous to read his work dissociated from his life. It does not seem interesting to make of Foucault's work a privileged exegesis of our analysis. We would, in this case, be making philosophy in a way that Foucault himself criticizes and puts into question in his last courses.

It is not the cast of doctrines, problems or concepts in the history of philosophy that interests Foucault the most, but the "history of the philosophical life as a philosophical problem" (2009: 196). This is what Foucault is looking for in Socrates and in the Cynics: philosophical heroes, not because of the assumed gleam of their doctrines, but because of the explosive, militant, and revolutionary character of their way of life and lifestyles; because of the force that they have to inscribe themselves critically and devastatingly in the tradition of how a philosophical life must be lived.

This is the philosophical problem that anguishes Foucault in his last moments: how to live a life that would be worth living, and how to situate life itself in the tradition of thought that will give a meaning and reason to the lifestyle itself. Socrates' life is the beginning of that tradition. The life of Cynics continues and deepens it: life is a scandal. It is the life of philosophy itself in its most profound expression, coherent, radical. It is philosophy made life.

On another level, the history of the philosophical doctrines is born with Plato and Aristotle. In it, the place of the Cynics is lesser. Nevertheless, if the history of philosophy was not dissociated of the philosophical practice, then the Cynical life is as outrageous, as essential, because of the radical, heroic and revolutionary way of living it. Foucault shows some moments of the history of philosophy—for example in Montaigne and Spinoza—in which that dimension is also distinguished, in a general background of negligence and oblivion. If that history was remembered and traced to nowadays, M. Foucault himself, his philosophical life, would deserve, without a doubt, a singular and essential place next to the philosophical lives of Socrates and the Cynics. If this history reaches the habitants of this side of the ocean, there is no doubt that the Venezuelan Simón Rodríguez, Caracas' own Socrates, would not be outside of this story. That is what we will try to justify in the next chapter. Who knows, maybe it is time, among ourselves, to think more seriously about philosophy and the history of philosophy in which we would like to see ourselves and our lives.

Bibliography

Foucault, M. (2001) *L'herméneutique du sujet*. Cours au Collège de France, 1981–1982. Paris: Gallimard; Seuil.

———. (2008) *Le gouvernement de soi et des autres*. Cours au Collège de France, 1982–1983. Paris: Gallimard; Seuil.

———. (2009) *Le courage de la vérité. Le gouvernement de soi et des autres II*. Cours au Collège de France, 1983–1984. Paris: Gallimard; Seuil.

Gros, F. (Ed.)(2002) *Foucault: Le courage de la vérité*. Paris: Presses Universitaires de France.

Hadot, P. (1993) *Exercices spirituels et philosophie antique*. Paris: Albin Michel.

3 Journeying as a way of living, endeavors

Simón Rodríguez

This chapter is an essay about life. It is about traveling. It is about life as a journey. In that sense, this essay can be regarded as part of a broader project for thinking about what could nowadays constitute a good life in the fields of education and philosophy in which we work. What would it mean, for example, to enjoy a good scholarly life, a good life as a professor, as a student? Moreover, how could a school, or at the very least, how could a classroom promote and foster different ways of good living? Let the reader notice that I am not striving "to teach what a good life is" nor "to contribute for a good life in society", but to practice a good life, to live a good life. The very division between life and school is part of the problem, for the former only enters the latter as an object of study or as a lecture topic. Therefore, in this chapter, with the guidance of Don Simón Rodríguez, we will seek to write about life and the good life with someone who has spent his life traveling, committed to the world of education, to school, to thinking and writing about the education that we need in Latin America.

Every time we write we assert life. There is always a life that is affirmed (and many others that are denied) when we experience a writing, whatever the subject or the purpose may be. There is no way to decouple life from writing. Nevertheless, when—such as in this case—life becomes the object of writing, when we write about life strictly in this context, about the life of a human being; we then affirm this life twice: in the life that appears written and in the life recreated by writing itself; in other words, in the life of that human being that twice becomes flesh in words, within himself and in the life that he takes on with each gesture of writing and reading. Another way of talking about this double dimension: life is as much as in what we can affirm in writing, and in what moves us to write, in what life gives strength and meaning to writing. It is the same for the readings that it generates. In that double relationship between life and writing, and in between life, writing and reading, we write and we write ourselves in a life.

Thus, I do not write to defend ideas or concepts, to pay homages or dry tributes, nor to consecrate thoughts, although something of this could also inhabit this act of writing. I am not interested in the word dissociated from the vital movement that pronounces and transports it where the conditions do not seem to be set for it to be heard. The word is important in the multiple move-ments of life and writing, in what it brings and generates from a life that was lived for the lives waiting to be lived starting with the reading of its writing. For this I write, for this I am writing.

Notice I wrote "the life of a human being" and not the one of a philosopher, educator, intellectual, or so many other things that could be used to describe an extraordinary and fruitful life such as that of Don Simón Rodríguez. I say "human being" because I want to avoid the specific modes of profession to find that life as bared and wholesome as possible. It is true, it is a bit stinging to write about someone who was given more than one name and was called by Simón Bolívar, his disciple, the Socrates of Caracas (Rodriguez, 2001b: 117). But it also produces a great temptation, especially because of the extraordinary power that emanates from such a quixotic life, exciting and passionate, dedicated to prob-lems, and what that life can make us think of present lives in this shared land. That life seems fascinating because it is good, because of the coherence and the summit in which it was lived. Also fascinating is his writing, which is envelop-ing, remarkable, irreverent. After having written about the Socrates of Athens (cf. Kohan, 2013) and Foucault's socrates, maybe it is time to find a Socrates closer in time and place, and why not? in life itself. Now it is time to write! With the vital and scriptural impulse of the Socrates of Caracas.

Still, it is necessary to make one more clarification. The reader should not expect a historiographical or hermeneutical essay. We are not interested in writing a biography of Simón Rodríguez, a difficult and polemic task indeed, of which there is a rich and plentiful bibliography already produced, that only in part we will include in the bibliographic references. Neither have we wanted to reinstate the principal ideas of this author, his theoretical contribu-tion, and his thoughts. It is not about interpreting, about saying what Rodríguez truly would have thought of education, about philosophy or about anything else. Of course, we will take many references from his works, but we will do so in order to be able to think along with the conceptual character, to search for inspiration in a life filled with thoughts, to try and feel the transpi-ration of a nomadic experience, inquisitiveness, originality, in search of a meaning for a life that we would like to live in education and philosophy. What we will try, above all, is to practice, essay, exercise in writing, practice in life and in thoughts just as Simón Rodríguez wanted. To travel through our thoughts, the way he traveled, so much, in life. Therefore, it would be a "Rodriguezian essay" in this exact sense, in which what inspires this writing is, maybe and excusing our pretentiousness, what used to inspire the writing and life of Don Simón Rodríguez.

I do so in a world, the academic one, that, as we were saying in the last chapter, has distanced itself from life. It has built its own world, its own rules, its own life, sometimes shaded, subdued, evasive, giving its back to the world of life. In the middle of that world we live. Quite an amount of life crosses that world. A lot is written in there. A lot is written about many lives. How much life lives in those writings? What type of life? In which way do these writings affirm or negate the life that crosses them? I wish not to be too pretentious answering my own questions. In any case, this writing inhabits that academic world and it does so wagering to the life that also circulates in that world. The one that it itself can also circulate. Attentive to the game of academic writing, we rely on it inasmuch as it helps us think about the educational value of a life much more than to validate the pedagogical truth written by that life. As we affirmed in the introduction, this is a book written as experience not as truth.

It is always possible to find in the work and life of an author some motifs that differentiate him, that show him under a more specific light, or that set him apart in his originality, irreducibility, and driving force. It is not about natural or essential brands that are there waiting to be discovered or unveiled. Neither are they fixed points that some good readers get to manifest and others do not. They are compositions between writing and reading, moveable points combined with the interests of a comment that, without hurting the bets and original meanings, get them to play productively in a new field of meaning where they are to be validated. Basically, this is the meaning of reading: choosing some distinctive notes and make them tremble until they no longer seem to be the same ones; nonetheless you cannot say that they are not the same.

This genre of writing is precisely a dialogic one in that exact sense: one that is the result of two thoughts put together. That one seems more passive because of its own established character and the other one more active in its role of waking in the other what it is being thought, is only an appearance. Thoughts interweave between each other, they infect and transmit each other, and one and the other come out different from the encounter, in another way, without being able to think the same way they used to before the experience of the encounter, or at least, without being able to do so in the same way they used to. This is how thought is generated: in that unfinished and infinite dialogue, a constant exercise of reading and writing that unfolds new roads for our thoughts to inhabit them.

In this case, we will read the life of Don Simón Rodríguez from the perspective of a few reasons that I judge powerful for thinking about what we are interested in thinking. They are probably not the only ones, the most important, the most essential ones, nor the most truthful ones either. There would be many others. There have been and there will be more. Perhaps in ourselves. I have chosen the ones that I will present next because I consider them to be faithful to a style of thought and life that we search for in this book. I say this again: there is no pretension in this writing exercise to reach the truth but to provoke the senses, senses that are measured in each reading, in what this writing is capable of provoking in its readers.

I present, then, this chapter based on five motifs that can be found in the work of Don Simón Rodríguez. They are as follows: "An essayistic writing", "A nomadic life", "We invent or err", "A teacher gives attention to everyone", and "An encounter with Socrates, Diogenes and Other Ignorants". It is simply an attempt to organize what could be presented in many other ways.

An essayistic writing

So extraordinary and complex is the writing of Simón Rodríguez.... So singular and powerful ... it is surprising, at first glance, in its form: letters different in size, space and font. Highlights and emphasis everywhere, bold, italics, brackets, braces, simple lines, double lines, charts, ellipses, repetitions, blank spaces. This aspect by itself gives meaning to the act of reading: it is worth reading Simón Rodríguez, if there were no other reasons—that surely exist, and in large numbers—because of this singular element that hinders any easy, fast and inattentive reading. Rodríguez does not write in the way we are accustomed to writing in a certain academic world with the standardized forms and uniform and undifferentiated fonts...

In *Luces y virtudes sociales* Rodríguez explicitly states the reason for his writing style with a striking clarity, also distinctive of his writing: "The style is a way of living" (2001a, II: 139). One exists inside that style and not outside of it; one exists in how we say what we say and not only in what it is said. One writes for different readers in different ways, times and reading styles. Rodríguez emphasizes something that seems obvious: it could not be written in a monotonous way, undifferentiated, invariable about different topics for other readers ... nonetheless, this is how we often do it.

In that turn of his writing is manifested a distinctive signature of the "caraqueño"[1]: his rebellious character, irreverent, unpredictable. At the same time, as in many other instances, that irreverence supports itself in a thought so simple as well as undeniable: we do not write the way we think, writing has become a part of a bureaucratic machine that distances us farther from demonstrating through it what we think and who we are. Of course, there are exceptional movements[2], but in a general way we have bureaucratized it, depersonalized it, made it monotonous. We have de-formed it, as if the only important thing is what we write about and not how we write. Also, in that gesture, Rodríguez shows his writing signature, his thought, and his life, the denouncement of what we are being, something quite far from what we want to be or from what we say we are being.

Therefore, the way in which writing expresses itself not only affirms different ways of thinking, but also contributes to the creation of different ways of reading. To be able to feel the tonality and style, it is necessary to read in the way it has been written. Simón Rodríguez describes it in detail (2001a, II: 158): without styles, writing unifies what it cannot be but diverse: size and variety of character indicates the tones, while the separation and isolation of phrases shows pauses; periods out of a phrase separates them, and when we draw a phrase in the middle of the page, we isolate it. Under an empty space, periods indicate an ellipsis; a hyphen, the relationship; braces, the connection. It is almost unacceptable that we have confined ourselves to a mono-form type of writing. On the contrary, the signs painted by Rodríguez constitute a way of writing and reading that remind us, in each stroke, of the inseparability of form and content. Some state, insistently, that what we write is never what we write only, and that how we write is an inescapable part of the exercise of transmission. In its own way and rhythm, Rodríguez's graphological writing forces us to ask fundamental questions such as: why do we write what we write? What do we want to generate with our writing?

That writing also shows us that the act of writing is a form of art, just as it is a more ample form of communicating, so much that "One could PAINT without TALKING but one cannot TALK without PAINTING" (2001a, II: 151)[3]. Let us say it one more time: one cannot talk without painting. Talking is an artistic gesture. When we are with others, our body communicates with gestures what words alone cannot; we paint the air with gestures. What it is said in an oral discourse is also valid for the written one: "The *art of Writing* needs the *art of Painting*" (2001a, II: 157). Writing is also an artistic gesture. Art is creation at the service of a major comprehension. In both cases, there must be connection of ideas and thoughts, of feeling and thinking. We write with our bodies, with gestures, with images to understand and to help understand. In the same way we paint. At the base of every act of writing, there is always a feeling. The challenge of the writer, Rodríguez claims, is to learn to express someone else's feelings, those that excite your own, because they are precisely the ones that excite your reading (2001a, II: 158). Through feeling, he persuades; making us think, he convinces (2001a: 153). One writes from his or her feelings and thoughts in order to get others to feel and think, convince and persuade.

Rodríguez differentiates two forms of writing: the aphoristic one for the well-informed readers and the didactic one for the not so well informed. It is not about underestimating. Neither is it about putting conditions but to adjust writing to the sensibility of a reader that can find in it what he or she is searching for, what he or she needs to live with others. One writes, in a strong sense, for everyone, the same way one is a true teacher for everyone (2001a, II: 17).

A nomadic life

Rodríguez was a foundling child, meaning his parents abandoned him at birth, at the end of October 1771[4]. It also means that from the beginning of his life he was exposed to walking, to wandering, to having to search and find a place[5]. His parents would have been Cayetano Carreño and Rosalía Rodríguez. He had a brother, Cayetano Carreño, also a foundling. They were both raised by an uncle, father Rodríguez, a respected priest, educated, with an ample library. Apparently, the brothers were quite different, not only by their last names, one belonging to the father, the other one to the mother, but because of their way of being in the world. His brother was a professional organist who never left Caracas. On the other hand, Simón Rodríguez had more than just a profession and, at the age of 26, he left Caracas to never come back[6].

From his first years, life would not be peaceful for Simón Rodríguez. He attended one of the three schools in the city, but because of being a foundling he could not enter the university. In any case, he must have had a good education under the wing of his uncle priest, which included the learning of languages and, above all, a direct contact with a rich library. By recommendation of the renowned teacher Guillermo Pelgrón, the town council of Caracas awarded him with the title of teacher at the age of around 20, in 1791. It is probable that by then he had a couple of years of pedagogical experience as Pelgrón's assistant. He takes his position right away, in the *Escuela de Primeras Letras [School of First Letters]*, a group of 114 children, 74 that pay and 40 that don't, nine of them, foundlings; the next year, in 1792, he becomes the teacher of orphan Simón Bolívar, with whom he establishes a deep relationship. In 1793 Bolívar attends the school where Rodríguez teaches, and for three months, he receives Bolívar as a pupil in his home.

The lives of Rodríguez and Bolívar crossed each other in many senses. They affect each other in a very singular, unquestionable and profound way. Had they not met, neither of them would be the way they are. In a sense, one cannot live without the other, although the years of coexistence had been some few years in total. The vital presence of the other one is felt as well as needed, essential, unshirkable. However, both lives can also be dissociable from each other; they have an existential density that does not reduce the presence of the other.

In 1794, Rodríguez addresses a public document to the city council of Caracas criticizing the *Escuela de Primeras Letras* and proposing a reform. The proposal is not taken up and Rodríguez renounces his position first and, later on, his city, beginning a series of trips that will never bring him back to Caracas. The reasons for his departure are not clear[7]. They are not necessarily in a direct relationship with this experiment, neither with a revolutionary movement in which some biographers argue Rodríguez takes part along with some Spaniards and half-breeds (in Spanish, "pardos").

There a new life starts. So much that it is necessary to change his name from Simón (Narciso) Rodríguez to Samuel Róbinson. He only keeps his initials, the beginning of the first beginning. The most apparent reason seems to be to protect himself from the eventual persecutors. But there are other more affirmative reasons. To change a name is to bet on a new identity, to be in a different world, to other forms of social life. It is a form of compromising with learning, with not knowing oneself as something definite, finished, regardless of the firm principles and profound convictions that one may have. That new name will accompany him for 26 years while he travels through Jamaica, the United States, and Europe, until he returns again to America, when he will keep traveling through Colombia, Ecuador, Peru, Bolivia, and Chile, this time with his former, birth name. In all the countries he visits he learns the native language, something that allows him to understand English, German, Italian, Portuguese, Polish, Russian, and French. What does he do in his travels? Little is known about his concrete activities; it is only possible to conjecture that he reads a lot in each place he visits, that he wishes to learn the most distinctive features of each culture and that he works every time he needs to, not a few times, as opposed to Bolívar, for he does not have a great fortune nor a family that supports him financially. Most of the time, he makes a living out of teaching.

In the United States he works as a typographer, in France, he opens a school in Bayonne to teach Spanish, French, and English. He leaves that school to open another one in Paris, with the Mexican Servando Teresa de Mier. And so on and so forth, in various European countries, he learns, reads, and teaches. On the other hand, there are not many records of his writing other than a translation of Chateaubriand's *Atala* and the drafts of some books that he will publish years later in America.

From Paris he travels to Vienna where he re-encounters Bolívar, with whom he goes back to Paris to spend three years together. They go to Italy by foot, where in Rome, at the top of Mount Sacro, they swore to free their homeland. They go back to Paris, where Rodríguez stays, when Bolívar decides to go back to South America. Apparently, Rodríguez does not feel secure enough to go back. He continues traveling. In Russia he directs an elementary school. None of his projects are for long periods, something that should not be understood as a failure. Rodríguez is an initiator, and inspirer, a punter. What is of interest lies in what occurs, in what it provokes, and not in a final product.

The journeys are already part of his life style. Róbinson creates an existence out of traveling, meaning that he does not live for traveling but travels in order to live. He finds his life in these journeys, on being on a journey, because being on a journey means to be on the road, in between two points, the point of departure and that of arrival, both of them equally unsatisfactory, almost unbearable, like places to reside for someone so restless. In traveling he feels at home, in a place for passage, of transformation, such as school, such as life, a place for learning. In traveling, he feels on the road to a new project, to a new beginning, to a new life. In traveling, Rodríguez finds Róbinson and the latter allows everybody, any attentive human to find him.

In London he finds Andrés Bello, with whom he will meet again many years later in Santiago de Chile. He opens a school again. He creates his own teaching methods. Always like this: he travels, he learns, he teaches. He stays in constant movement. He never stops traveling. He does not want to arrive to any place in particular. His homeland is not Venezuela, not even America; perhaps the world.

Yes, perhaps the world. If there is no life in other worlds. In 1823 he decides to go back to America[8]. He does not do it because he is American but because he wishes to carry out a libertarian project that he has shared with Bolívar. And because he considers it a favorable land "for attempts and essays" (2001b: 141). Rodríguez is a cosmopolitan, a "member of the Human Society" (2001b: 187) someone for whom "my homeland is the world, and all men are my partners in misfortune. I am not a cow to have attachment, nor native to have misfortune" (2001b: 201). When he returns to America, he arrives at Cartagena, Colombia. He goes back to his former name. To the first one. He looks for Bolívar to help him carry out their communal oath made in Rome. It is not easy for Rodríguez to find him. Bolívar is in Peru, and while he waits to meet him, he opens a school at a hospice.

If we do not have a lot of precise data about his schools in Europe, the situation is different about his first school after he returns to America, denominated "Casa de Industria Pública" [*House of Public Industry*]. It is a school for the people, the poor, the ignorant, the classless or illegitimate. It is a school of training for life and for work, open to the immense majority of the excluded "bogotanos"[9]. But the conditions are not met, and Rodríguez encounters problems with his local interlocutors. He feels misunderstood and treated like a madman (2001b: 141). He knows it from the start, but he does not stop trying. He cannot stay still, passive, inactive. He always prefers to risk, to dare. He always plays out and he compromises himself, even when the conditions are not hopeful. He will do his *mea culpa,* but he will never stop preferring to do something imperfect before waiting for the ideal conditions for his work to be carried out.

When he feels like there are no more conditions for him to keep trying, he abandons the project to go in search of Bolívar in Peru. After the mutually desired encounter in Lima, they travel together to Arequipa and Cuzco, where they open a school for girls of "any class". In La Paz, they inaugurate a library. In Chuquisaca, then capital of Bolivia, Rodríguez presents the "Educative Plan" for the country and he is named Director of Public Education and of many other issues.

Once again, Rodríguez and Bolívar separate. Even though there are clear reasons that explain the separation, we might consider that some important tension between them made them part and later on Rodríguez felt this separation with tremendous regret. Bolívar returns to Lima because of strategic reasons, and without him, Rodríguez cannot put his ideas into practice: shortly thereafter, he writes to Bolívar to inform him that the project has failed. He does not get along with Sucre and with the rest of the people with whom he must work. Six months later, when he travels to Cochabamba to create new schools, the model popular school just built in Chuquisaca is shut down. He feels like an inventor ahead of his time. Failing to understand the principles and the meaning of a popular education—the education of the poor and classless of both sexes for work and life, to constitute the citizens that the republic needed with the people of its own land, stripped of their own—they accuse him of sheltering prostitutes and thieves. For Rodríguez, to educate is to give back. The defenders of the establishment react violently. They give back the oligarchical class what was invested in the education of the people. They leave more than 2,000 matriculated children and about 1,000 former street beggars defenseless (2001b: 193).

Rodríguez is distorted in the eye of public opinion and is declared mad. As always when he feels misunderstood, he does not confront his opponents and chooses to leave in silence. He strongly desires to go back to Bolívar, not only for himself, but because he feels that they need each other. He goes to him, but Bolívar has already departed to Colombia and hence, they will never meet again. His financial conditions worsen gradually since he never makes a profit out of his projects. He makes a living out of his labor, and although he works and writes tirelessly, his projects take all the money. He remarries with a Bolivian indigenous woman named Manuela Gómez with whom he has two or three children.

In 1853, he travels to Lambayeque, in Peru, with his son José and a friend of his, Camilo Gómez. While sailing in a fragile boat, he suffers a serious accident due to the currents. He relapses in the town of Amotape, where he dies in February 1854, at the age of 83.

We invent or we err

The alternative that gives the title to this section cuts across the life and work of Simón Rodríguez as a scream, as an expression taken out of his core and chewed by a life of thought and work dedicated to education. The alternative is always one and the same: on one side, creation, invention, thought, life, and liberty; on the other side, reproduction, error, imitation, opinion, servility. The former is what we need and we do not practice in schools in Latin America. The latter one is what we have been doing until now, and revolves around the notion of transformation. The transformation of schools, and the subsequent education of the people, of the owners of this land, is nothing but the road for such transformation.

This alternative appears to be set out in various ways, in many contexts, as an answer to a whole variety of issues, at different moments. It is a philosophical, pedagogical, political and existential alternative. It is there where our existence is at stake, and where the project of what we could be lies. Acidly, in a letter of July 20th 1845 (2001b: 185), the Republican Ecuadorian system emerges as a bad copied parody of the English constitution. It is about "*thinking*" instead of "*copying*". The proclamation is repeated time and time again when he writes about the public instruction for America, that "It should not imitate obsequiously, but be original" (2001a, I: 234).

There are several reasons to hold up that flag. The first one being that, in America, none of the modern States have done what they should: truly educate the people, in knowledge and in doing, for a communal upcoming life, inaugural, unprecedented. Rodríguez is not an Americanist in the strict sense of the word, and the opposition between particular and universal seems to be a misleading binary opposition to approach his thought. Simón Rodríguez is both things at the same time. What he wants for America he also wants for the whole world, and the inventive that he asks for America is justified because what it needs does not exist in any other place. There is no educational system to copy, there is no State that assigns to education the money that should be assigned, there is no basic education that opens its doors to all the people that they should be opened to. There lies his radical and intransigent critical character. There is not a Republic that has the schools that a republic should have. Schools function in Europe almost as bad as in America. America must invent its own institutions and its education, because

the institutions and the education can account for the problems that constitutes the American reality, a reality that, at the end of *Sociedades Americanas,*
published in 1842 (2001a, I: 193ff.), can be summed up as follows: a) there
should be bread for everyone, there should be no hunger; b) justice adminis-
tration, empire of peace and dialogue; c) an educational system that teaches
one to think, that is, to have intellectual sensibility, to establish all the necessary
relationships to understand an issue; moderation, to occupy oneself in what is
important to take care of socially, to stop worrying about things that do not
matter, and to leave a free path for the nourishment of the ability to create.

There are more reasons. It is necessary to invent because to imitate means to
reproduce the structure of submission and extermination that has been reign-
ing for centuries in America. The learned logic in the monarchic schools is an
example of that. It is there where sophisticated reasoning abilities are learned
in the form of the Aristotelian syllogism to thus conclude that they have to
beat indigenous with sticks to make them work simply because they are not
men (2001a, I: 243). The use of such logic is unacceptable in America (and in
any other place). It is necessary to think above other foundations, to think by
feeling, to think by painting a reality of liberty for all the people that inhabit
these lands. Truth is not out there waiting to be discovered. Truth is part of an
ethic and a set of politics that would make this part of the world a place of real
freedom for those that inhabit it, a place like no other on earth.

Thus, either we invent or err. Invention is the criteria of truth, an epistemological and political support of the life that we are affirming. Not all inventions
are truthful, but we know that if we do not invent them, we cannot access the
truth, that truth cannot be imitated, reproduced, copied, or modeled from
another reality. We have to find truth by ourselves, or else we will never find it.
How can we find truth by ourselves? How do we invent ourselves? For this,
Rodríguez trusts in the creation of new schools for social education. But the
answer to these questions is not easy nor is it written in a book. Rodríguez's
own life is the attempt to think about them.

A teacher gives attention to everyone

A teacher is someone that helps another person find what he or she is. Can
teachers do this in schools? Should they do it? The relationships between
teaching and institutions are complex and dynamic. In schools teachers fulfill
the social role that is expected of them, roles that can be in conflict with what
is postulated in the former statement. However, Rodríguez thinks that both
alternatives can be given in school. Moreover, he thinks that if in the existing
schools both are irreconcilable, in the ones that he himself would institute with
his proposal of popular education, not only would these be compatible, but also
that the first meaning of what being a teacher is all about—helping others to
find who they are—would be nothing but the path for the second to be
achieved, so that, in this way, schools fulfill their distinctive function within a
republican society.

Let's see how Rodríguez thinks about these meanings more specifically. He differentiates a series of roles or pedagogical functions. There is a main difference between instructing and educating, or between teaching and educating. In the first case of said alternative, one transmits knowledge; in the second case, one teaches how to live. The ones that do the first are "bocinas" [horns] (2001a: 233), teachers who take pride in a knowledge that they themselves do not even know how to utilize. One can be very wise and lead an unworthy life. There are enough examples in the times of maestro Rodríguez: "As proof that by accumulating knowledge, alien to the art of living, nothing has been done to form the social conduct – we could look at many wise men, badly raised, that populate the country of sciences" (2001a, I: 104).

The education that America needs, that Rodríguez refers to as general education, popular or social, is exactly the one that integrates knowledge and life, the one that teaches people to live (2001a, I: 106), which translates to teaching people to be active, animated, autonomous. According to this idea, it is all the people, without exceptions, the ones who must constitute the world of knowledge, of thought, of action. An educated nation is a nation uprightly educated, in which everyone thinks about others and not only about themselves. Nobody is educated in a society in which there are people, even if it is only one person, without an education. This is also another reason why America has to invent itself and not imitate, that is why it makes no sense for a country to bring European immigrants without first educating its own people from childhood. If we imitate Europe, we will imitate an uneducated society, with millions excluded from education, and therefore, from a social world.

A parallel distinction accompanies the previous one between "lecturer" and "professor". The first one transmits knowledge; the second one instructs for life in society. The former is the one who knows about a topic and communicates it, from above; anyone can do this, all we need is to prepare ourselves with a minimum of previous studies and to recite the knowledge in question. The professor, on the contrary, is the one who "lets the others see, through his dedication, that he or she applies him or herself exclusively to the study of an art or a science" (2001a, I: 246). This last one receives in other writings the name of teacher, a name about which we can distinguish three different types: that which resolves to show that he knows and thus does not teach, in other words, the conceited one; that which wants to teach so much that he confuses his disciples (these two types would be a form of "catedrático" or "bocina" teachers); and lastly, "others that put themselves at the reach of EVERYONE, they consult with him for his capacities. These last ones are the ones that achieve the goal of teaching, and the ones that perpetuate their own names in the schools" (2001a, II: 17).

That is, teachers in the existing schools act like "lecturers" but not like teachers. Not only does the act of being a teacher require knowing the principles of knowledge but also to be able to "help to study", to "teach to learn", and most importantly: "to get one INSPIRED, and to EXCITE in others, the DESIRE to know" (ibid.). Put differently, that the teacher is not the one who transmits what he knows, but the one who generates the desire to know, the one that inspires in others the desire to know. Teacher is the one who provokes in others a change in their relationship with knowledge, the one who takes them out of their apathy, comfort, illusion, thus making them feel the importance of understanding and understanding themselves as part of a social whole. Ultimately, it is the one who creates the conditions so that the desire to know for understanding and transforming life can be born in others. It is the one who instills on the will of the apprentice his own desire to learn, the one who works on the attention of the apprentice so she can pay attention to her life and what he/she needs to know to live in a different way with those whom she shares her life. Does the reader remember Socrates as I do?

The art of teaching has three parts, attests Rodríguez (2001a, II: 161), and each one of those parts constitutes a way of working on the attention of the student: it is all about calling it, capturing it, setting it down. This is the difficult art of a teacher, because attention is "one and INDIVISIBLE" (2001a: 406). The teacher must go in search of her student's attention, must go out and meet this attention to seduce it, incite it and invite it to place itself on what is to be questioned, understood, thought about, and invented—that is, to get attention to tend to what it is that life needs to live. Put in those terms, the work of a teacher is of intellectual sensibility with regards to the intellectual sensibility of the student. Does the reader remember Jacotot as I do?

Of the teacher, Rodríguez also states that he must be "wise, educated, philosopher and communicative" (2001b: 206). The teacher knows but does not teach what she knows; instead, she teaches the desire of wanting to know and understanding what is known. In this case, he is the one that "teaches to learn and helps to understand" (2001a, I: 246). Rodríguez specifies it in various ways: that teacher is not the one who forces to learn, neither is he the one who points out what has or must be learned; that is, he does not worry so much about what is learned by the learner; instead, he takes care that others never stop learning. This is what he knows the most, a knowledge for others, with others: when the others learns what he teaches, a relationship to knowledge—that is when knowledge is materialized and acquires coherency, when the others learn to live, to know how to live. The teacher then thinks of others and not of himself, if he searches for knowledge it is so that the other ones can know. This teacher must be at the beginning, at the elementary school, he is the one in charge of establishing the first relationship of those who learn with learning, because by learning what he teaches, or better yet, that relationship that he teaches through learning, is what gets them to learn everything else, and without that learning nothing could be learned that is it worth of learning.

A teacher who deserves this name educates, with art, everyone with no exceptions (2001a, II: 104). He is the teacher of the people, of a popular and general education, of a social school.

An encounter with Socrates, Jacotot, Diogenes, and other Ignorants

When one traces a painting of a thought it is a temptation to compare that painting with the thoughts of others. The richer the thought, the bigger is the temptation. I will approach some figures that were present in previous chapters. Simón Bolívar himself called Rodríguez the Socrates of Caracas. There are at least two references in this context in the respective letters that Bolívar sent to General Francisco de P. Santander. In the first one, sent from Pallasca on December 8th 1823, he claims to know of Rodríguez's return from Paris, and asks Santander to give Rodríguez, on his behalf (Bolívar's), the money that he needs. He literally affirms that his teacher: "Is an accomplished philosopher, and a patriot like no other, he is the Socrates of Caracas, although in a falling-out with his wife, like the other one with Xanthippe, so he is not missing anything Socratic" (2001b: 117).

The tone is very commendatory, of admiration. Of the fall-out with his wife we have no other information. It is possible for Bolívar to have as a basis for this a series of intimate conversations in Europe, common between friends. In truth, neither is there much information about the confrontations between Socrates and Xanthippe. And even though the phrase closes with an affirmation of complete similarity between the two characters, there are no other elements in that letter to understand Bolívar's basis for supporting such an accomplished similarity.

The other testimony is even fainter, in another letter that Bolívar sent to Santander, this time on May 6th 1824, from Huamachuco. The letter is full of praises for Rodríguez, of whom Bolívar says: "He was my teacher, my traveling partner, and he is genius, a Prodigy of grace and talent for those who know how to discover it and appreciate it" (Rodriguez, 2001b: 122). The eulogies continue and after a very long paragraph Bolívar concludes: "I have the necessity to satisfy these manly passions, since the illusions of my youth have been turned off. Instead of a lover, I want by my side a philosopher, because in the day, I prefer Socrates better than the beautiful Aspasia" (ibid.). As it can be seen, Bolívar repeats the descriptive term of philosopher and traces an indirect analogy between Rodríguez and Socrates. Here, the comparison is not justified either, and there are no other explicit testimonies.

On what can this comparison be based? In some aspects there seems to be a distance that cannot be disguised. Let's see. Socrates almost never left Athens, unless it were for some military missions, while Rodríguez was an incorrigible traveler. Socrates only spoke Greek and he demanded others to speak his language, while Simón Rodríguez learned and spoke fluently at least six languages (English, German, Italian, and French besides Spanish and not counting Latin). Socrates did not write anything, he did not trust writing, he went for oral dialogue while Rodríguez was a writer obsessed with publishing his ideas (it is also true that his publications were mostly after Bolívar's letters). Socrates states to not have been anyone's teacher, and

Rodríguez takes pride on having been Bolívar's teacher. Socrates did not create any institution, and Rodríguez founded an endless number of teaching schools and institutions. Socrates claimed to be wise for not knowing anything and Rodríguez demonstrated countless knowledge. We could trace other differences, but these seem enough and important to establish a certain distance between the two.

It is not about concealing or negating that distance, yet one cannot deny either that the similarities are more than visible. J. D. García Bacca (1978: 12–23) has pointed out personal aspects in the likeness: in the character, both energetic, arguers and defenders of their ideas, proud, unbreakable, even similar in the physical appearance: robust body, protuberant features, sarcastic smile. García Bacca also shows the similarities in religious matters (Socrates was accused of not believing in the city's gods and it is also known the "extravagant" ideas that Rodríguez had in religious matters) and in their way of dying: both died (and lived) poor and had a lucid death (Socrates talking to his friends about life, death, immortality of the other world; Simón Rodríguez giving a materialistic dissertation to the priest Santiago Sanchez, who went to visit him). García Bacca concludes his comparison reinforcing the similarity between them as "models of simplicity", that in the sense that they both knew how and when to dress up (Socrates in the *Symposium*; Simón Rodríguez in a portrait that is being kept at the Military Academy of Quito (García Bacca, 1978: 21)).

The portrait of García Bacca is precise. We want, with all this, to add something more. Perhaps in Bolívar's testimonies other things carry more weight, for example, a way of living in common, a similar posture in front of himself and others that could be summarized in the Socratic *dictum* of the *Apology* ("an unexamined life is not worth living for a human being", Plato, *Apology of Socrates*, 38a) and of which Simón Rodríguez finds himself so closed to that he seems to have embodied it in a life of permanent questioning and the search for himself and for others. It is impossible to deny that the ways in which each set forth on that search acknowledge differences that, among other things, cannot put aside the cultural distance and the time period. Nonetheless, both Socrates and Don Simón fit well in the analogy that the former one makes about himself as a horsefly, whose mission would be to wake up the citizens from the dream that they live in.

Socrates and Rodríguez are strong critics of the societies of which they are part, social disturbers who have a pedagogical project to change society. Even with all the differences, both of them share an obsession for finding the other people to "educate them". For both of them the time of teaching others to live has come. And both of them are betting completely on it. The second accusation against Socrates was that he "corrupted the youth". The same thing fitted Don Simón, whether it was corrupting spirits of the privileged class, like Bolívar, or educating about liberty when speaking to those that were instructed to obey[10]. They are misunderstood, considered exotic, foreigners in their own city and, when they are understood, they are judged as dangerous to the established order. The Caraqueño had, perhaps, a little bit more of luck than the Athenian, but could have easily been killed in the attempt.

In addition, they both think similarly about the role of the educator: both of them look to distance themselves from the teacher who transmits knowledge and they present themselves as inventors, each in their own time, of a new place for the educator and a new meaning for education. That place has to do with the awakening of the others of a way of life that seems unworthy, that does not seem like life. They are equally irreverent in the way that they do it. Each of them invents his own methods, his own way of doing what they do.

They both look to bring others out of their ignorance, to change the relationship that their fellow citizens have with knowledge, so they can take care of what they do not take care of, so they can think about what they do not think of. Socrates differentiates himself from the professional pedagogues of his time by not charging, by not transmitting any kind of knowledge and by not changing his public or private discourse. Rodríguez would later on ascribe himself to all of these things, although he did have to charge occasionally to be able to survive.

It is possible that, examined in much more detail, many differences come to the surface. All in all, I believe that it is worth paying attention to that common philosophical, pedagogical, and political gesture of facing, with no concessions, the values affirmed in the state of affairs, of being both intransigent critics of the social way of living. They both seem to include their own lives in this gesture. One cannot separate life from teaching out of their lives. One cannot separate life from the ones that learn what they learn, but neither can one separate one's life from what one teaches. Socrates and Rodríguez teach *themselves* in their teachings. Both of them live to teach and teach to live.

Without stepping out from the Greek world, García Bacca has also compared Simón Rodríguez to Diogenes the Cynic. In the same manner, in this case, the cultural and historical differences are notorious, but García Bacca symbolizes a common characteristic in the disdain towards the arrogant attitude of the tyrant. In the case of Diogenes, he remembers the anecdote narrated by Diogenes Laercio, according to which when faced with the visit of Emperor Alexander the Great, Diogenes asked him to leave so he could take a sunbath. From Rodríguez, he recreates the scene shared with Bolívar at Napoleon's coronation, when teacher and disciple escape the coronation party and lock themselves in a room with closed windows to isolate themselves, this being the most intense form of showing disdain towards the wretched crown.

There is also an anecdote used by García Bacca that serves as the basis for a good analogy. It is said that Diogenes was in Athens with a lantern lit up in full daylight in search for a man. In a portrait of one of Rodríguez's disciple, "A Guerrero en Latacunga", of 1850, the teacher appears walking and holding a lantern at the bottom part of his cane, searching, Garcia believes, for the "American man".

The comparison can go in depth, inasmuch as Diogenes radicalizes in a way the Socratic gesture of foreignism and irreverence. In Diogenes, his life is his truth; there is barely a dialogue, method, pedagogy, unless it deals with the display of oneself, to life itself, raw, bared, as a gesture that is at the same time pedagogical, political, and philosophical. If Socrates and Simón Rodríguez, are teaching life itself, their own life, then Diogenes could not be different because there is no other thing to teach. The scandal comes in this case entirely from his body itself, erected in a pedagogical act.

The similarities with other European thinkers contemporary to Simón Rodríguez's time are tempting. There have been a lot of speculations about the influences that he received during more than 20 years on European soil, about his readings and encounters. Usually, they emphasized the influence of Rousseau's *Emile.* We have not located anything about Joseph Jacotot, the French pedagogue to whom J. Rancière has given life through *The Ignorant Schoolmaster,* as we considered in a previous chapter.

With Jacotot, Rodriguez seems to have shared his occupation for the poor and excluded ones. Both of them think about an education for the rejected ones, the ones upon whom the effects of an education at the service of the dominant's way of life, in Europe and America, are felt more. Both of them work in education to invert that situation. By the way, there is a fundamental difference: after some "failed" attempts, Jacotot arrives to the belief that emancipation can only be given from individual to individual, that there is not such a thing as a social emancipation, the one that Rodríguez had worked for all his life and in which he always trusted, beyond the experiments that never succeeded. There is, in this case, an unavoidable opposition: Jacotot ends up affirming an incompatibility between institution and emancipation that Rodríguez will emphatically reject.

Despite all of this, there are points of common interest. Both of them have the pretension for universality; they believe that education must care for everyone, without exceptions, that it cannot exclude anyone by right in the field of knowledge, of thought. Both of them trust in the abilities of each human being, in governing the life of each one the least possible, and in generating the condition for that potential to materialize in everyone, with no exceptions. Both of them think that an educator who appreciates all that will work on the will of those that learn, since the will is the engine of thought. For the two, to educate is to create wills. Although they have developed specific and precise methods for themselves, none of them seem to give much importance to them. They both share the idea that each teacher should choose their own path, and that the real fight goes through the principles and the meaning of their labor.

There is in Rodríguez an explicit criticism towards ignorance that seems exalted by Jacotot. But both thinkers work in two conceptual levels with ignorance. In the case of Jacotot, if it is true that he emphasizes the teacher's ignorance, he also does it to stress the disassociation between knowledge and teaching. In other words, it is about founding the role of a teacher in something different to knowledge. Jacotot's teacher is a teacher not because he knows, unless what he knows is the equality of intelligence. The ignorance that Jacotot takes most into account is a political one and not epistemological: the ruling ignorance of inequality in the institutional order. It is more a disobedience than an ignorance in the strict sense. The emancipative teacher knows inequality and does not want to know anything about accepting it; he ignores it in the sense of disobeying it. There is not praise *stricto sensu* of ignorance, but a political role of ignorance in relation with the inequality of intelligences.

Simón Rodríguez would not have many problems in accepting this principle and such political value of ignorance. He also works with ignorance on two levels. On a more superficial one, the term seems to have a more colloquial absence of knowledge, but on a deeper level, one can see it functioning as the lack of wanting to know, of will of learning (2001a, II: 118). The ignorant is not so much the one who does not know but the one who cannot and does not want to know, and, for this same reason, cannot govern himself. Ignorants can think of themselves as being well educated but, because they have lost completely the curiosity, which is the engine of knowledge, they are completely incapable of governing their life based on what they know. This is why Rodríguez searches for the elimination of ignorance, and this is why he fights it as one fights an enemy. Seen under that light, ignorance would also be an enemy for Jacotot.

Among the Latin American educators, the similarity perhaps more pointed at would be the one between Simón Rodríguez and Paulo Freire, the Pernambucan educator, known as an outstanding figure in the frame of the so-called "popular education" or the "pedagogy of liberation"[11]. Although there are no testimonies that Freire actually read Rodríguez, some of his categories-words seem inspired in the "Caraqueño". This is the case, for example, of the "inédito viable", that echoes Rodríguez's call to invent and to never accept the given as finished, fulfilled, unmodifiable; or of curiosity, as the engine of education and life. The same could be said about the happiness that accompanies necessarily the educational act, in the figure of the educator and in his own way of living a life dedicated to education (Freire, 1996: 72). Here, also, it seems that the "Caraqueño" teacher is smiling in the shadow of the Pernambucan.

There are other common aspects between S. Rodríguez and P. Freire that come to the surface at first glance. Among them we will highlight: the communal sharing of a popular education, and the work of both of them in favor of the most socially excluded; the commitment to the exercising of a governmental position within the realm of public education in Latin America; their valorization of school as the ideal institution to produce the desired social changes; their defense of teachers' working conditions as a requirement for the well-functioning of the educational institution; their criticism towards the methods and the "traditional" teaching systems, and their proposal of methods and alternatives ways of teaching, this is, the reinvention of the role and the meaning of the educator (for both, the methods are not valuable on their own but for the goals that they pursue); their traveling spirit that went across

America and Europe thinking and acting in favor of education; their trust in words, speech, criticism, argumentation, dialogue, and reasoning as a form of pedagogical and social relation.

I could specify other aspects, yet I would rather stop here and explore in depth some of them, something that will allow us to see some deep similarities and also significant differences. Before I continue, it is perhaps convenient to appreciate a new similarity: here we are talking about two living human beings, thoughtful, restless, who have played all their cards in favor of the act of thinking, and who have thought in different ways in different moments of their lives. I mean to say that, in the case of Paulo Freire, the distances, for example, between *The Pedagogy of the Oppressed* and *Pedagogy of Autonomy*—just to make reference to two of his most famous works—are notable. Therefore, the first question that emerges almost immediately at the moment of relating these two thinkers is: which Rodríguez and which Freire are we relating to here?

Without overlooking the importance of that question, we will trace a parallel with the purpose of allowing ourselves certain freedoms to circulate in different moments of Freire's work. The case of Rodríguez is simpler, since we will refer only to his work written in America, after his return from Europe. With this framework, it is worth thinking that although it may well be true that both of them affirm a clear and explicit commitment to the education of the most excluded ones, they also settle on different ways. While Paulo Freire concentrates his efforts in the literacy of the popular class and, more specifically, of adults and peasants, Rodríguez focuses more on the intellectual and the vital formation of children and the rejected children of the young cities of South America that he lived in in the first half of the nineteenth century. In a way, in Rodríguez's mind both reading and writing—privileged acts in Freire's pedagogical action—are stages that are secondary to his formation, that is, secondary to the learning of calculus, logic, thinking, and argumentation (the spoken word). For Freire, on the contrary, the literacy of youth and adults is the key that will allow them to carry out a critical reading of the world as a nodal tool for the transformation of one's self and the world. There is in that a horizon of investigation and work in the education of thinking: how do we learn to think? Rodríguez and Freire are two privileged and differentiated interlocutors to think about this question.

In the *Dicionário Paulo Freire* (2008: 40–1), Carlos R. Brandão states that among the human beings who travel, there are those who do it because they want to (travelers, tourists), others do it out of belief (pilgrims), others because they need to (exiled ones, the hungry ones) and, finally, the ones who travel because they have to (the committed ones). He affirms that Paulo Freire belongs to the last two categories. We believe that so does Simón Rodríguez. Both of them are incorrigible travelers, for necessity and conviction, for commitment and coherence. As anecdotal as it may seem, we may also mention the fact that they coincide in some of the countries in which they lived, such as Bolivia, Chile, United States, and England. With all this, even on common ground, the motivations for their trips perhaps are somewhat different, the commitment and necessity to nourish themselves from different sources. Freire is forced to exile by a dictatorship, first in Bolivia, then in Chile and later in Europe (England and Switzerland) because his own life is in danger after a military coup in Brazil in 1964. Rodríguez, as we saw, did not have this urgency to set on a journey, despite the mythic and heroic story about his assumed participation in the Gual and España Conspiracy against the Spanish monarchy. Rodríguez is not a revolutionary and that is why he travels; nonetheless he becomes a revolutionary when traveling, in travels. Even his relationship with his homeland is very weak: he never goes back to Venezuela and it is exactly outside of his country, while traveling, where he finds the motive and a meaning for his commitment with the excluded ones. In the case of P. Freire it is very different. His relationship with his homeland is carnal, and as soon as the political conditions allow it, he goes back to Brazil in 1979, to stay there definitely. His revolutionary commitment, with the excluded ones, has always been there, from his contact with poverty and oppression in his native Pernambuco. His travels reinforce in a way that commitment and it makes him a cosmopolitan. In his exile, he travels around all the continents: Africa, Asia, Europe, Oceania, and America … from his work as a Special Consultant of the Department of Education of the World Council of Churches.

This detail deserves attention. Even when persecuted in his country, P. Freire is recognized internationally, appointed as a professor in many prestigious universities such as Geneva and Harvard, he occupies important public positions in the Department of Education in Chile, and in UNESCO, and he also has an important institutional link with the Catholic Church, all of which is absolutely absent from Simón Rodríguez's life, who serves as the minister of education of Bolívar in Bolivia for a few months only, but who before and after is almost marginalized from the laical and ecclesiastical institutions, to the ones that he frequently opposes and the ones by which he is belittled and scorned. Freire, on the contrary, has occupied an important place in some of both. His first adult literacy jobs take place in the *Movimiento de Educación de Base*, within the influential *Conferencia Nacional de Obispos del Brasil* (CNBB). He always maintains a very close relationship with the most progressive sectors of the Catholic Church and with the movement of Liberation Theology. In the same way, he participates in the founding of the Workers' Party and occupies the position of Secretary of Education in Sao Paulo when he returns from exile. He is named Doctor *Honoris Causa* in many universities of Brazil and other countries, many cities designate him an honorary citizen, he receives a countless number of prizes, his books have been translated in more than 20 languages and many other prizes and tributes are instituted in his name, in his honor. Rodríguez's life is marked, on the contrary, by the lack of recognition and he was only recently valorized even in his own country. His iconoclastic character marks his traveling life in America: he lives in the most absolute state of poverty, scarcity, and ostracism. In an epoch of major clerical power, Rodríguez was anti-clerical until the last moment.

In his famous controversy with I. Illich (Freire and Illich, 1975), P. Freire clearly states his position with regards to the educational institution that holds a strong proximity with the one of S. Rodríguez. Although it is true that he shares with the Austrian thinker his criticism about traditional schools, Freire nonetheless defends the role of the new school for social transformation. Even when considering that one can learn in many different ambits besides school and advocating for the creation of alternatives spaces such as the "Círculos de Cultura", Freire conceives, just as Rodríguez did, school as a place to fight for, as a place of hope, one of the engine for a political and transformative action.

In any case, the main proximity between these two characters has to do with the meaning of education: both of them are educators for the transformation of the state of things. Beyond language, and the affirmed categories—not in vain, in between the two went Marx, whose influence is explicit and notorious, particularly in the *Pedagogy of the Oppressed*—there exists a profound community when we think of education in its social and political dimension. In this sense, for both of them, education constitutes a commitment impossible to avoid with the popular class, the deprived ones. If there is not education for the excluded ones, there is no true education. For Freire, particularly in *Pedagogy of the Oppressed,* that true education supposes, above all, to unmask the ideology of the oppressor, to make the pedagogical act, a fundamentally political act that will free the oppressed one from his condition of his inhumane life and to nourish his vocation, epistemological and ontological, to know more, to be more. This is, first and foremost, about acquiring conscience, about consciousness, to develop, through the educational practice, a critical thinking that will allow to wake, in the interior of the oppressed, the contradiction that he himself unwillingly reproduces, the political reality in all its complexity of its praxis, that is to say, a reflection that will make it pass from the alienated conscience to a transformative action of itself and of the world. For this, the educator performs a crucial problematizing function: to problematize students with regards to their own condition, at the same time that they problematize themselves (Freire, 1983: 74 ff.). Nothing could be more similar to the pedagogical thought of Simón Rodríguez than Freire's belief regarding the critical function of education, to the necessary connection between theory and practice and the role of educator, even the criticism of Paulo Freire to education and the banking educators, transmitters of a knowledge or techniques that are not theirs and that, when they do not problematize, they reproduce with their assumed ideological meanings. The affinity sharpens even more when Freire emphasizes that the pedagogy of the oppressed in its second moment it is not only of the oppressed but of all men in the permanent process of liberation (Freire, 2005: 47).

Although we could bring in other characters, we will stop here. In the end, it is about essaying in thinking as well as in writing and in the reading. Simón Rodríguez, Socrates, Diogenes, Jacotot, Freire, people of thought and actions, of words and life, different, strange, enigmatic, will all perhaps help us think in our time. Each of them in their own time, in different ways, all of these characters have been considered crazy, foreigners, childish. "Children and madmen speak the truths," repeats Simón Rodríguez over and over in his *Extracto sucinto de mi obra sobre la educación republicana* (2001a: 221 ff.). Also, he repeats more than once, that it is about educating children to be inquisitive. It is time to ask then, who insists on negating these truths of children and madmen? Who clings on to belittling the truth of thoughts and life of Don Simón Rodríguez? Let's give these questions a more affirmative form: who dares to think with these questions of a life for the education of our time? Who dares to invent, to invent oneself, to invent for ourselves a life in education inspired by some of these madmen? Who dares to make school guided by Don Simón Rodríguez's hand?

Notes

1 This is a demonym used to refer to a person from Caracas.
2 Within those movements we could cite, as an example the work of Marshall McLuhan, *The Medium is the Message: An Inventory of Effects* (New York: Bantam Books, 1967), or the concrete poetry, both closed, among many other examples, in the spirit, to the ambition of Rodríguez.
3 I leave Rodríguez's original spelling, as much as possible, with his capital letters, bolds and italics.
4 Some biographers date his birth 1769. It does not seem possible to definitely clarify this matter.
5 Biographers adscribe a different importance to this event. M. Álvarez does not see anything special in it, inasmuch as the law, according to her, used to assimilate the foundlings to the legitimate children (1977: 17). A. Uslar Pietri (2009) sees there an effect of universality that makes him a son of nobody, a fact that allowed him to be called in any way and to be son of any high-class mother from the city. C. H. Jorge (2000: 63 ff.) makes of this a fundamental element to comprehend all of Rodríguez's work.
6 More precise details can be found in the introductory essay of his *Obras completes [Complete works]*, by A. Rumazo González, "El pensamiento educador de Simón Rodríguez", 2001a, I: 21–132.
7 For the following, see Durán (2012).
8 By America, Rodriguez refers to what we would now call "Latin America". I maintain his expression to help the reader think in the plurality of meanings of the word.
9 This is a demonym used to refer to people from Bogota.
10 García Bacca highlights this aspect with particular emphasis and elegance. When referring to the quote "Dénseme muchachos pobres" de *Sociedades Americanas de 1828*, he writes: "This is what being a teacher and a director of education with social cosmopolitanism is all about" 1978: 33.
11 In this sense, a classic reference would be the work of Adriana Puiggrós, 2005.

Bibliography

Álvarez F., M. M. (1996) *Simón Rodríguez tal cual fue*. Caracas: Ediciones del Cuatricentenario de Caracas.
A.a. V.v. (2012). *Simón Rodríguez y las pedagogías emancipadoras de Nuestra América*. Montevideo: Editorial Primero de Mayo.

Dicionário Paulo Freire (2008) Danilo R. Streck, Euclides Redin, Jaime José Zitkoski (Eds). Belo Horizonte: Autêntica.

Durán, M. (2008) "Infancia y Hospitalidad en Simón Rodríguez", *Childhood & Philosophy*, Rio de Janeiro, v. 4, n. 7, p. 83–102, jan./jun.

——. (2011a) "La supuesta influencia de Rousseau en el pensamiento de Simón Rodríguez: La tesis del *Emilio*", *Iberoamérica*, Revista del Instituto iberoamericano de Berlín, a. XII, n. 42, pp. 7–20.

——. (2011b) "Radicalidad y originalidad en el proyecto de educación popular de Simón Rodríguez", *UNICA*, Revista de Artes y Humanidades de la Universidad Católica de Maracaibo, v. 12, n. 3, pp. 85–105.

——. (2012) "Simón Rodríguez: militante de una idea", in A.a. V.v. *Simón Rodríguez y las pedagogías emancipadoras de Nuestra América*. Montevideo: Editorial Primero de Mayo, pp. 73–101.

Freire, P. (1983) *Extensão ou comunicação?* São Paulo: Paz e Terra.

——. (1996). *Pedagogia da autonomia*. São Paulo: Paz e Terra.

——. (2005). *Pedagogia do Oprimido*. São Paulo: Paz e Terra.

Freire, P. and Illich, I. (1975) *La educación*. Buenos Aires: Búsqueda.

García Bacca, J. D. (1978) *Simón Rodríguez. Pensador para América*. Caracas: Ediciones de la Presidencia de la República.

Jorge, C. H. (2000). *Educación y revolución en Simón Rodríguez*. Caracas: Monte Ávila.

Kohan, W. (2013) *Socrate. Ensegeiner: ce paradoxe*. Paris: L'Harmattan.

Lasheras, J. A. (2004) *Simón Rodríguez. Maestro Ilustrado y Político Socialista*. Caracas: Universidad Nacional Experimental Simón Rodríguez.

López P. J. (1989) *Simón Rodríguez. Utopía y socialismo*. Caracas: Universidad Central de Venezuela.

Ortega, F. A. (2011) "Tomen lo bueno, dejen lo malo: Simón Rodríguez y la educación popular", *Revista de Estudios Sociales*, Bogotá, n. 38, pp. 30–46.

Prieto C. D. (1987) *Utopía y comunicación en Simón Rodríguez*. Caracas: Academia Venezolana de la lengua.

Puiggrós, A. (2005) *De Simón Rodríguez a Paulo Freire. Educación para la integración latinoamericana*. Buenos Aires: Colihue.

Pulgar M. C. (2006) *La materia y el individuo*. Estudio literario de Sociedades Americanas de Simón Rodríguez. Caracas: El perro y la rana.

Rancière, J. (1987) *Le maître ignorant*. Paris: Fayard.

Rodríguez, S. (2001a) *Obra Completa*. Tomos I-II. Caracas: Presidencia de la República.

——. (2001b) *Cartas*. Caracas: Ediciones del Rectorado de la UNISER.

Rosales, S. J. J. (2008) *Ética y razón en Simón Rodríguez*. Caracas: Universidad Nacional Experimental Simón Rodríguez.

Rozitchner, L. (2012) *Filosofía y emancipación. Simón Rodríguez: el triunfo de un fracaso ejemplar*. Buenos Aires: Ediciones Biblioteca Nacional.

Rumazo González., A. (1976). *Simón Rodríguez: maestro de América*. Caracas: Universidad Experimental Simón Rodríguez.

——. (1980) *Ideario de Simón Rodríguez*. Caracas: Ediciones Centauro.

Uslar P. A. (2009) *La isla de Róbinson*. Caracas: El Nacional.

Part II

Philosophy and a childlike education

4 Philosophy and childhood
Possibilities of an encounter

In one of its dimensions, philosophy is a practice that problematizes dominant ideas, beliefs and values. In effect, all through our experience of the world, we notice dominant orders and, at the same time, flaws or discontinuities in those same orders. No social domain is ever completed or fully self-sufficient. Wonder, suffering, bother are unique human feelings that emerge from sociability. From feelings like these, philosophical questioning and investigation are nurtured. In this sense, philosophy might be considered as an attempt to overcome the immobility of the dominant social orders.

It might be understood that this attempt is developed in two complementary forms. As a critical task, philosophy questions values, ideas and faiths that permeate the practices socially dominant. At the same time, as a creative task, philosophy sets conditions in order to think and propose other orders, alternatives to the actual ones. As criticism, the dispositions and methods of philosophy are exercised on all significant practice to de-construct its ordinary, routine or daily character. For philosophy there is no natural need, nothing normal or obvious in the human experience of the world. Every norm, value, knowledge, belief can be understood in terms of a historical arrangement produced after a long contest. Therefore, it is always extra-ordinary, contingent, controversial. Then, criticism is the path to creativity in that it settles down the conditions of possibility to think new states of things. In that double movement of questioning and establishing conditions to propose alternatives for a certain dimension of reality, philosophy spreads itself out in a varied group of "philosophies ...": of mind, of language, of culture, of religion, of education, of sport, of technology, among others, count among the groups most valorized in our contemporaneity.

Critical and creative philosophies of childhood

At least for the last 40 years some philosophers, like M. Lipman (1993b) and G. Matthews (1994), have been defending the right of childhood to be constituted in one of those areas of interest for philosophy. Lipman himself went farther, not only giving theoretical foundations to the need of this field (1993b) but also creating and taking into schools a pioneering proposal that reconstructs the history of philosophy in such a way that it can be practiced by children.

Others like M. Benjamin have been marking the inconvenience of such a domain (1993, passim). Benjamin presents, basically, two reasons: i) an area like "philosophy of childhood" would end isolated by itself (in developing a highly shut language and technique) and also by other areas of philosophy, that would ignore it; ii) the existence of a separate area "philosophy of childhood" would violate the integrity of human life, atomizing it or breaking into fragmentized compartments.

We consider these arguments to be inadequate: it is not philosophy of childhood that atomizes the integrity of human life, but the productivity of practices of confinement, subjectification and exclusion that exist, independently of whether philosophy reflects on them or not. The sub-discipline of philosophy, philosophy of childhood, is an effect of recognizing those practices, not its cause. Were the historical productivity of the relationship adulthood/childhood less significant, perhaps a philosophy of childhood would have little meaning or sense. But it is not the case. Phenomena like child abuse, child prostitution, child labor, street-children and alike implore a gesture of thinking, so that philosophy not only doesn't generate the atomization of human life, as Benjamin suggests, but it can become a tool to overcome it or, at least, to rethink it in terms of its assumptions and consequences. In relation to the eventual isolation of the new discipline, this is clearly tied up to the way it is developed, and it doesn't constitute a necessary character of its existence. Benjamin is probably thinking of other "philosophy of …" that have developed a technical language so that only a chosen few are able to follow its discussions and elaboration. In other words, philosophy of childhood could not take the same path of the other sub-disciplines of philosophy that have been dramatically separated from her other sisters by the sophisticated jargon developed by academic philosophers.

Corresponding to the conception of philosophy roughly characterized in the first paragraph of this chapter, to foster a philosophy of childhood would imply, at least, two dimensions. A first one, critical, is founded in the need of recognizing, understanding and questioning values, knowledge and ideas that underlie and sustain the social productivity of the idea of "childhood". In other words, what social dispositives in our contemporary world make the actual idea of childhood historically possible (its conditions of possibility), what developments make it understandable in the history of humanity (its historical place), which are the assumptions underlying this idea (its theoretical support), and which are its effects and consequences in the social life of our time (its social productivity). A second one, creative dimension, in which other values, knowledge and ideas, alternative to the existing ones, are affirmed concerning the idea of childhood, complements the critical dimension.

Let's expose this idea a little more. In our daily life, words like "child" or "adult" are presented as common, normal, simple. It is presented as obvious that some people **are** children and others **are** adults; it is shown as natural that some activities and forms of relationships among human beings and to the world are specific of children and not of adults. Expressions such as "These are not issues that children should be part of", "You are 12 years old. You should not be so childish" or "You are always playing. You are not a child any more" denote this kind of attitude. From their first years, children learn to include themselves in a specific class, from which they need to go out as soon as they can if they want to be adults. In an inverse way, there exists what is forbidden to children with the argument that it belongs exclusively to the adult universe. "You cannot do that. Those are things for older people," it is said.

Nevertheless, as we have already suggested, philosophy is, precisely, the placement in question of the "normality" or "naturality" of the human experience of the world. It recognizes no necessary law or order in human societies. "It would not necessarily be like that" a philosopher might say. In terms of our theme, philosophy problematizes the normal ideas concerning childhood and adulthood. In fact, these ideas could be absolutely un-natural to, let's say the Greeks, the Egyptians or the contemporary Musulmans as their "natural" ideas sound extremely unnatural to Western culture. What is considered a child, what is expected/unexpected, allowed/forbidden, rewarded/punished/in children, changes, due to cultural and historical issues. Social roles addressed to children are significantly different through time and space. In such a sense, from P. Ariès' pioneer and controversial work (1973[1960]), a series of studies developed in the field of social history to affirm the modern genesis of the actual dominant idea of childhood (Baquero and Narodowski (1994: 65). In the framework of a more general process that occurs slowly through the fifteenth to eighteenth centuries, a series of social dispositives and techniques of individualization and totalization are progressively established to normalize and discipline individuals, to turn them in to subjects as M. Foucault has already established in his late works, in the double meaning of the word "subject": "someone who is subject to someone else by control and dependence, and tied to his own identity by a conscience or self-knowledge" (1983: 212). In the case of childhood, children have been exposed to social practices, dispositives and techniques that subjectivize them in the space of the other-ness, the alter-ness, the mis-valued, the incapable, the excluded and the explored. This subjectivity is expressed in different spheres of the social life: the cultural, the economic, the epistemic, the aesthetic, the ethical, the juridical, the political (cf. Kennedy, 1997, passim).

As soon as we recognize the arbitrary in the natural, the contingency in the necessary, the extra-ordinary in the ordinary, philosophy finds its place. Our own thinking is transformed, things cannot be seen any more the way they were seen. Recognizing those characters enables us to consider social change not only as desirable but as imperative. Particularly, the supposed naturalness that surrounds the idea of childhood loses its strength and we find fertile field to ask, for example, "what presuppositions and implications have, here and now, splitting human beings into children and adults?", "how is the limit between both categories based?", "which are the cultural, economic, epistemic, ethical, aesthetical, juridical and political consequences of being considered a child in front of the ones of being considered an adult?"

There are no children by nature. Neither there are adults by nature. This social categorization is linked to practices, knowledge and values that constitute identities, give shape to interpersonal relationships and structure ways of life. In the detection, understanding and problematization of the knowledge, practices and values that underlie and are inferred by the child–adult division is the basis of the critical dimension of a philosophy of childhood. In other forms of thinking about those categories, lies its creative dimension.

This double task can be divided in to several spheres, each corresponding to a different area of philosophy. D. Kennedy traced the first lines of a road in the theory of knowledge identifying what he denominates the "gnoseologic adult egocentrism" (1995: 42). In effect, after recognizing the need to recuperate children's excluded voice, Kennedy argues that such purpose will not be achieved, showing that children can think as well as adults. On the contrary, the first step should be to recognize that what he calls "the hegemonic theory of knowledge of the day" or the "rationalistic ideal of reason", systematically excludes children's thought and experience. Only after deconstructing that dominant theory of knowledge will it be possible to reintegrate what inhabits the children's *episteme* that has been silenced in the adult rationality.

In the other fields of philosophy it is possible to look for similar movements to the one suggested by Kennedy. The different spheres of development of critical and creative philosophies of childhood emerge when it is put into question what the adultism has been infusing in philosophy: the dominance and absolute empire of an adult aesthetics, ethics, metaphysics and politics that subjectivize children as the inferior other, someone that still is not an entire being, for whom to be themself means to be what others have thought for them to be, that do not have appropriate conditions to choose for themself what they want to be.

As Kennedy suggests, this critical task, paradoxically, most of the time is developed by other academics rather than by professional philosophers. A book by G. Matthews (one of the philosophers with larger academic prestige in the field) gives an example of what we are trying to say. In a text that intends to base the field of the philosophy of childhood, Matthews mentions the philosophically problematic character of the concept of "childhood" (1994: 8) and affirms that "the difficulties genuinely philosophical appear only in the way of saying what type of difference is the difference between children and adults" (ibid.). Matthews tries to show how, in different fields (literature, art and philosophy itself), children are not so different from adults as these believe. In all of those cases, according to Matthews, the differences between children and adults are insignificant and children could very well enter and share the adult's world. Children, concludes Matthews, are not so far away from the paradigm of adult rationality.

As we already said, the philosophical task concerning childhood is not only to see what type of difference is settled down between children and adults but also how this difference is valued, what presuppositions sustain that valorization and what consequences follow from it. Matthews proposes to include children in the adults' own rational world, without questioning the hegemonic practices, values and knowledge, therefore legitimating the actual dominant rationality and closing space for any eventual alternative world. The "promising" inclusion of children among the world of the adults does not allow to distinguish social dispositives of exclusion and subjectivation and dismantles the appearance of any different rationality. What might children expect from this "generous" inclusion in adults' rationality? Their adaptation as "outsiders" to the center? A non-recognition of their "otherness"? A silence of their voices as children?

Philosophy and children: an encounter

The forms of the encounter between philosophy and children are not reduced to the philosophies of childhood. About 30 years ago, M. Lipman inaugurated a movement (*philosophy for children*) to incorporate children to the world of philosophy. What can children and philosophy expect of this encounter?

What philosophy can give to children is one of the favorite topics of the theoretical writings of Lipman. According to Lipman, the contribution of philosophy to children is multiple: on the one side, philosophy is a practice of thinking *in*, *among* and *about* the other disciplines that enriches the meaning of the whole educational experience (1991: 264; 1993b: 148) of children; on the other hand, it is a tool that allows them to rich autonomous and higher order thinking that in that way leads them to an improvement of their judgments (1991: 262–3). In such a sense, philosophy becomes a defender of a democratic education, when generating a political understanding and a reflexive education of concepts (like justice, freedom, person and alike, the "eternal" themes of philosophy) that affect children's daily experience, as well as when promoting a space of dialogical and rational deliberation of those subjects in the classrooms (the community of philosophical inquiry, 1991: 244ff.). Thus, philosophy contributes to children in supporting an education practice based on values like democracy, dialogue, inquiry, thinking, reasonableness (rationality tempered by judgment).

The contribution of children to philosophy is a subject less explored by Lipman. However, he has highlighted at least four fields of philosophy that would achieve valuable consequences through this encounter with children: the philosophy of law would be enriched by the current discussion on children's rights; the effective capacity of children to engage in ethical inquiry would have important repercussions in the land of ethics; the actual formation of children's communities would illuminate social philosophy and, finally, in philosophical anthropology the understanding of the question "what is a child?", would throw light on the question "what is a person?" (1993b: 144). Even though Lipman also mentions a fifth territory, philosophy of education, he does not, however, explicit what would be its benefits.

The main purpose of Lipman's argument is to protect and to legitimate for children and childhood a place in philosophy. This encounter would also have significant social repercussions: it could contribute to mitigate "the ignorance, irresponsibility and mediocrity that now prevails among the adults" (1993b: 148). Finally, Lipman suggests that "to treat the children as people can be a small price to pay, long term, for some more substantial social achievements" (ibid.).

As we see, Lipman provides pragmatic, social and political reasons to recognize children as persons, human beings endowed with full rationality. According to Lipman, if philosophy treats childhood and children as equals, good results will occur not only for them but for philosophy itself, as well as for the forms of social ways of life.

Although Lipman's proposal is inspiring, it doesn't drain the possible consequences of the encounter between children and philosophy. Now, starting from the program *philosophy for children* created by Lipman, thousands of children all over the world are already inside philosophy. Children from three years old, at places as distant as Buenos Aires, Melbourne, Budapest, Montclair or Duque de Caxias, are having a philosophical practice at school. They are appreciating philosophy from its inside. Finally, philosophy has included children as subjects of philosophizing. In spite of that, their income to philosophy has only been as individuals or groups. It is licit to wonder if a more stable and structural insert of children will not appear more deeply in philosophy. It is legitimate to wonder if philosophies *of* children of another nature than traditional philosophy, with a similar group of questionings to it will not appear in the future.

We are allowed to venture this possibility because from their philosophical practice many children are improving their capacity to recognize, understand and value the different dimension of living a life of a child. They are learning to wonder and problematize what it implies to be considered a child in their time and place. In fact, their philosophical practice has been actually producing critical philosophies of childhood.

Let's consider just a short example. Some years ago, at a Public School of Brasilia, the Federal District of Brazil (304N, Plano Piloto, Brasilia, DF), a group of 9-year-old children was discussing with their teacher about how they could contribute to solve the problems they experienced at school. After a quite thorough debate where some alternatives were considered the children evaluated their discussion. When the teacher asked them what they had learned, one of the kids said: "I learned that not only adults decide but children also decide."

What has this child learned then? That children "also decide". It is interesting to notice that he does not say "children have the right to decide" or "children can decide". He says "children decide", reflecting an actual capacity that has been exercised during the class of philosophy. He learned that children can decide because children have been deciding during that class. Therefore, not only adults decide in this world. This child verbalizes a dominant order ("adults decide"), challenges it ("not only adults decide ...") and conceives an alternative one ("children also decide").

What this child expressed shows the kind of empowerment philosophy offers to children. From philosophy itself, a lot of children are enriching substantively the understanding of their position in the social world they inhabit. And they are also increasing their appreciation of the presuppositions and consequences of being considered, even by themselves, an imperfect or incomplete version of adults. In summary, *philosophy for children*, as the actual practice of philosophizing with children in schools and other contexts is helping children to progressively acquire a better understanding of that form of gnoseological, aesthetical, ethical, social and political dominance named "ageism".

While disposing philosophy to children, *philosophy for children* has actually produced a rupture with the adultocentrism that has been dominating in philosophy for more than 25 centuries of history. For the first time, children have frank and open access to the practice of philosophy. Newly, philosophy says to children: come here, you're welcome, feel at home, there is something we can work out together.

This incorporation of children to the universe of philosophy, facilitated by *philosophy for children,* re-creates conditions to think questions like "what is a child?" and "what is an adult?", as questions historically and socially posited, from an aesthetics, an ethics, a politics, and a rationality no more monopolized by adults. More, by the process it has been generating, *philosophy for children* is fostering conditions so that children themselves could produce creative philosophies of childhood. Therefore, conditions are being settled and practices are being developed toward the appearance of philosophies of children, movements that might break the adult omni-dominance in philosophy.

Children themselves will build their philosophies and their methods of producing them. It is not by showing that children can think like adults think that we will revoke the absence of their voice in philosophy. On the contrary, in that case we would have co-operated to co-op them to a different voice, what constitutes another form of silencing them. It would be more appropriate, to get ready to listen to a different voice as expression of a different philosophy, a different reason, a different theory of knowledge, a different ethics and a different politics: that voice historically silenced for the simple fact of emanating from people stigmatized in a "non-adult" space.

The eventual appearance of the philosophies of children has consequences that are going besides the space of philosophy. Such philosophies will recognize, comprehend and put into question knowledge, practices, and values that cross the world of the identities and relationships between children and adults. Thus, they will be a force pushing for unexpectable changes in the most diverse social domains.

Philosophy of childhood and the philosophies of children

In this chapter, we have been using at least three expressions to link children to philosophy. They are "philosophy for children", "philosophy of childhood" and "philosophy of children". In the following section, we'll clarify them.

The first expression, "philosophy for children", gives form to a pioneering initiative, created by M. Lipman, to take philosophy (with its classical themes, tools and methods) to children. It is a way to reconstruct the whole history of Western philosophy, disposing it to children. Lipman himself has created a curriculum from pre-school to high school and it has been practiced in more than 30 countries for the last 30 years. Actually, *philosophy for children* has led to a "philosophizing with children" where they become co-participants of a practice based on philosophical questioning and inquiry. This philosophical practice with children (independently of one's acceptance of the peculiar dispositive of texts (novels and manuals) and methods proposed by Lipman) is giving place to philosophies of childhood and it will probably be the vehicle for the appearance of philosophies of children.

The second expression, "philosophy of childhood", intends to mean a philosophy applied to a given phenomenon, concept, idea or dispositive, historically and socially located: childhood. The historical conditions for the appearance of this discipline are tied up to the invention, in modernity, of childhood as a prolonged state of the human life that should be separate from the adult maturity. We propose a critical and creative character as normative of a philosophy of childhood.

The last expression, "philosophy of children", designates a movement that, it is to be expected, expresses the children's voice in different problematic ambits: an aesthetics, an ethics, a metaphysics, a social and political philosophy today absent in the dominant philosophical speech.

Philosophers will listen to those voices or will continue participating in a discriminative and excluding practice. In the first case, they will accept that the many differences between children and adults, as much as the many differences between women and men, back and white, and so many others, are irrelevant in terms of any form of discrimination in the realm of thinking. They will pass by this from a condescending and hierarchical relationship to a reciprocal and equal one. The presupposition of this idea is that age (as gender, race and others) cannot legitimate relationships of excludance and dominance.

Certainly, we won't do a great favor to children inviting them to paint in the watercolor of philosophy if we don't allow them that to enter with their screens, their inks, their paintbrushes and, above all, their own way of painting and of conceiving the art of painting. Certainly, it might be that they enjoy and have a good time with our paintbrushes and our inks. They even can become specialists in them and feel that they do not need to find their own ones. Even so, probably, it might also happen that they feel that those instruments are a little strange to them, that when adopting them they are confined by the creations of others, and those are not good enough to express themselves. But, in any case, we need to facilitate for children the conditions so that they can think what kind of painting they want to experience.

What children need of us, teachers, professors of philosophy, philosophers, is space for them to think, therefore to create. To impose on them our creations and our way of creating is to impose on them our experience of the world and to impede them of developing their own experience. To generate conditions so that children can paint their own watercolor of philosophy and of the world is, perhaps, one of the largest challenges for us who share this idea of bringing closer children and philosophy.

In the following two chapters some elements will be given to consider what education is about when it is sensitive to a philosophical approach to childhood. In other words, conceptual elements will be provided in order to put into question "traditional" ways of thinking about the relationship between childhood and philosophy in an educational set, as presented in this chapter.

Bibliography

Ariès, Ph. (1973 [1960]) *L'Enfant et la vie familiale sous l'ancient regime* (2nd ed.). Paris: Seuil. (1st ed.: Librairie Plon).

Ball, S. J. (ed.) (1990) *Foucault and Education. Disciplines and Knowledge.* New York: Routledge.

Baquero, R. and Narodowski, M. (1994) "¿Existe la Infancia ?", *Revista del IICE*, III, no. 4, pp. 61–6.

Benjamin, M. (1993 [1981]) "Comments on 'Developing Philosophies of Childhood' ", in M. Lipman (ed.) (1993a) *Thinking Children and Education.* Dubuque, Iowa: Kendall. pp. 149–51.

DeMause, Ll. (ed.) (1974), *The History of Childhood.* New York: The Psychohistory Press.

Foucault, M. (1983) 'The Subject and the Power', in H. Dreyfus, P. Rabinow (eds) *Michel Foucault. Beyond Estructuralism and Hermeneutics.* Chicago: The University of Chicago Press, pp. 208–26.

Kennedy, D. (1995) "Review to Matthews, G. (1994)", *Thinking. The Journal of Philosophy for Children*, vol. XII, no. 2, pp. 41–4.

———. (1997) "Reconstructing Childhood", paper presented at the VIII International Conference of Philosophy for Children, University of Akureyri, Iceland.

Lipman, M. (1988) *Philosophy Goes to School.* Philadelphia: Temple University Press.

———. (1990) "Response to Professor Kitchener (1990)", *Metaphilosophy*, vol. 24, no. 4, pp. 432–3.

———. (2001/1991), *Thinking in Education* (2nd ed.). Cambridge: University Press. (References are from 1st ed., 1991).

———. (ed.) (1993a) *Thinking Children and Education.* Dubuque, Iowa: Kendall.

———. (1993b [1981]) "Developing Philosophies of Childhood", in M. Lipman, (1993a) pp. 143–8. First published in *Thinking. The Journal of Philosophy for Children*, vol. III, (1981), pp. 4–7.

Lipman, M. and Sharp, A. M. (eds) (1994 [1978]) *Growing up with Philosophy.* Dubuque, Iowa: Kendall/Hunt.

Lipman, M., Sharp, A. M. and Oscanyan, F. (1980 [1977]) *Philosophy in the Classroom* (2nd ed.). Philadelphia: Temple University Press.

Matthews, G. (1993) "Childhood: The Recapitulation Model", in M. Lipman (ed.) (1993a) *Thinking Children and Education.* Dubuque, Iowa: Kendall, pp. 154–60.

———. (1994) *The Philosophy of Childhood*, Cambridge, Mass.: Harvard University Press.

Nandy, A. (1987) *Traditions, Tyranny and Utopias. Essays in the Politics of Awareness*, Delhi: Oxford University Press, Chapter III: "Reconstructing Childhood: A Critique of the Ideology of Adulthood", pp. 56–76.

Postman, N. (1982) *The Disappearance of Childhood*. New York: Delacorte Press.

Sharp, A. (ed.) (1994) *Thinking. The Journal of Philosophy for Children*, special double issue: "Women, Feminism and Philosophy for Children", vol. XI, nos. 3–4.

5   Childhood, education and philosophy

Notes on deterritorialization

Philosophy and childhood education: the traditional relationship

Childhood has been a privileged object of pedagogical utopias of various sorts throughout the history of Western educational thought, which goes back at least as early as Plato's *Republic*. In Book II of that treatise, Socrates suggests that the education of the guardians of the *polis* is essential in order to guarantee a just community, and that the genesis or cause (*aitia*) of justice or injustice lies in education or its absence (II, 376d). When discussing which stories should replace the traditional Homeric and Hesiodic ones, Socrates affirms (II, 376e–377b) that the first years of life are the most important, because all that comes later will depend on those first steps. This is what makes childhood extraordinarily important, because of the indelible marks that are received in those first moments of the human life cycle (II 378e). For this reason, special attention will be given to those first stages by the designers of the Republic, not so much for what children are but for what they will become.

In the *Republic*, it is someone external—the educator, the philosopher, the legislator of the *polis*—who will give form to another who in himself has no form, and who is not considered capable of finding it by himself. To give someone a form; to *in*form him: education is understood here *tout simple* as the formation of childhood. In this approach, education is normative, adjusting what is to what ought to be. According to this orientation, children represent adults' opportunity to carry out their ideals, and education is considered an appropriate instrument for such an end.

In this context, not only education but philosophy itself is understood as in the service of the formation of the young. Certainly, philosophy is not to be taught *to* children because, according to Plato, they are not capable of such a complex form of knowledge. But the knowledge that philosophy entails will inform the best natures, those of the most rigorous character (VI, 503b), those who are capable of becoming the best rulers because they are the best (*aristós*). In this sense, the learning of philosophy as kind of knowledge will facilitate the best formation of those best natures who by rights ought to govern the *polis*.

Although they may differ significantly in the details of their approach to education, to philosophy, and to childhood, certain contemporary programs that propose to educate children through philosophy, such as *philosophy for children*, maintain a similar relationship between the three terms, in that the educational potential of philosophy is justified on the basis of its utopian political force. Philosophical education, whether of the child or adult, and whether conducted through instruction or communal inquiry, is defended on the promise of its formative potential for a better world. Whatever the differences in their specific agendas, the fact remains that all these programs consider philosophy to be an educational vehicle that carries a political component (the Form of the Good in Plato, democracy in *philosophy for children*) useful for the optimal formation of the citizens of the *polis*. Thus, according to Matthew Lipman (1998) the logic of democracy (understood as deliberative inquiry) determines the purposes and meanings of the teaching of philosophy. To bring philosophy to children with its history, its methods and its themes is justified for the social advantages that such a practice will create (Lipman, 1988: 198). If a more solid or authentic form of democracy is desired outside schools, democratic practices must be established in them and developed through them. Children are educated through communities of philosophical inquiry in order that they be shaped into the democratic citizens that society needs. Again, if philosophy is incorporated into childhood education, it is because of the formative benefits of exposing the young to this form of thinking and speaking.

Alternative concepts of childhood

How might education be considered and practiced if not under the logic of the formation of childhood? More specifically, how might the purposes of practicing philosophy with children be affirmed other than as toward the social and political education of childhood? This complex issue calls for a redefinition not only of philosophy and education, but of childhood itself. The traditional form of the philosophical education of childhood that I have just described is constructed in keeping with a conception of childhood as a stage of human life. But the history of pedagogical ideas reveals different images of the child, some more positive, some less.

In fact, I would suggest that each conception of childhood presupposes a concept of time. Childhood as a stage of life presupposes a chronological concept of time: life is conceived as a sequential and consecutive line of movements. Time is the number of these movements. From this approach, Plato defines *chronos* as "the moving image of eternity (*aion*) that moves according to number" (*Timeus*, 37d). Time understood as *chronos* is only possible in the imperfect and ever-moving world of birth and death. The perfect world of Ideas is static, ana-chronic, aionic. Some chronological time later, Aristotle defined *chronos* as "the number of movement according to the 'before and after'" *Physics* (IV, 220a)[1].

In his fragment 52, Heraclitus introduces a different relationship between the child and time with the use of the time-word *aion*: "Time [*aion*] (is) a child childing (playing); its realm is one of a child". In its more ancient uses, *aion* designates the intensity of time in human life—a destiny, a duration, an un-numbered movement, not successive, but intensive (Liddell and Scott, 1966: 45). There is a double relationship between time and childhood in this fragment: time does what a child does (*paizon:* plays) and in time, as *aion*, child-hood governs (*basileie* is a power word, meaning "realm"). Thus, this fragment can be read as showing that time—life-time—is not only a question of numbered movement (*chronos*). There is another dimension of living time more akin to a childlike form of being (*aion*), non-numbered. In relation to this kind of time, a child is more powerful than any other being. In aionic life, childhood does not statically exist in one stage of life—the first one—but rather goes through it, powerfully, as an intensity or duration. In this fragment a non-chronological, aionic experience of time emerges and, together with it, a non-chronological concept of childhood. Childhood may here be understood, not only as a period of life but as a specific strength, force or intensity that inhab-its a qualitative life at any given chronologic time.

Deleuze and becoming-child

Many contemporary philosophers have offered us new concepts and vocabu-laries with which to think non-chronological concepts of childhood, a few of which I will take up in this chapter. My aim is not so much to establish any specific connections between and among them as to sketch a framework that allows space within which alternative ways of relating childhood, philosophy and education might emerge. Gilles Deleuze, for example, proposes an imper-sonal notion, a non-subjective form to which he gives names like "becoming-child" or "block of childhood". "Becoming-child" is not a matter of age but of flux, intensity. It is a revolutionary space of transformation. It is not that a given subject becomes a child, transforms himself into a child or lives a child-like life: rather, he occupies a space of transformation. In effect, "becoming-child" has the form of escape lines—"lines of flight" that cannot be incorporated or co-opted by the system: disrupted movements, changes of rhythm, segments that interrupt the logic of the state of affairs and intersect and divide it, with different roots and targets.

According to Deleuze (1990)[2], becoming opposes history. History gives the set of conditions in order that an event or experience can take place, but in itself, an experience or event is beyond history. An experience becomes, or emerges, it cannot be anticipated or planned in the successive moments of history. On the one hand there is the continuous—history, *chronos*, contradic-tion, dialectic, and the majority; on the other, the discontinuous, becoming, experience. Becoming-child is always in the minority, because being majority or minority is not a question of number, but of whether a model is being followed or not. Minorities cannot be numbered or grouped; lacking a model, they are always in process (Deleuze and Guattari, 1980: 585 ff.). The dynamism of minorities resides in their nomadism, which for Deleuze and Guattari (1980: 455 ff.), is a kind of acceleration aimed at escaping control, discipline, and any pretentions of unification; Deleuze characterizes this force of resistance as an "exorcizing [of] shame".

Besides distinguishing between history and becoming, Deleuze privileges geography over history, in an ontology that is replete with planes, segments, lines, maps, territories, movements. He proposes (1991) a geo-philosophy, a philosophy of the earth. Here, thinking is not a matter of subject and object, but "the relationship of territory and the earth", which creates the plane of immanence, where thinking takes place. In fact, thinking traverses diverse planes of immanence. Human beings also simultaneously traverse different, opposed, parallel, intersecting spaces[3]. On the one hand, there are the spaces of macro-politics, of the state—molar segments, binaries, which are concentric, resonant with each other, and are expressed by the paradigm of the tree, with its principle of dichotomy and axis of concentricity. On the other hand, there are the spaces of micro-politics—molecular segments, the rhizome, where binaries are multiplicities, circles are not concentric, and where becoming–child emerges. In this space, becoming–child is a war machine against the state and adult institutions. As the non-chronological time of becoming, it represents a space of resistance, a source of creativity and of experience of a different world.

In summary, Plato invented a plane of immanence on which to think childhood as a matter for social transformation through education, and to think education as the formation of childhood. On this plane of immanence, various images of childhood have been drawn, corresponding with diverse political and ideological agendas. As I have suggested, *philosophy for children* in its founding movement was also established on this plane. But new planes can be created in order to think philosophy *between* childhood and education, and Deleuze offers elements of a particularly provocative one.

Lyotard and infantia

Jean-Francois Lyotard offers yet another plane of immanence on which to think childhood, and from a very different perspective. According to Lyotard (1997), childhood represents the difference between what can and what cannot be said—*infantia* (literally "absence of speech") is for him the unsayable, or as he puts it, "what is not said" (Lyotard, 1997: 13)[4]. This childhood has nothing to do with a stage of life either, nor with something that is formed, corrected or overcome over the course of a life. Rather it inhabits, imperceptibly, the sayable as its condition, its shadow, or remainder. Consciousness and discourse attempt to deny, to efface *infantia*, but in this very movement they constitute it as something that is missed. Seen in this way, childhood is understood, not as a stage of language acquisition, but as a latent condition that inhabits every word that is pronounced—not just the words of children, but the words of every human being. To use another image from Lyotard, it could be said that childhood is a survival, an entity that should be dead but is *still* alive (1997: 63); childhood passes as infancy, but survives as *infantia*.

Infantia is the state of the soul "inhabited by something to which a response will never be given" (1997: 69). This something is a debt acquired by the fact of birth itself, a debt owed by the newborn to the other, incurred in order that the birth could happen, emerging from non-being, the other of being, what remains forgotten after birth. Childhood keeps alive this forgetfulness of an initial and constitutive debt that each human being carries. The initial non-being out of which every human being is born—this emptiness manifested by the absence of decision or consciousness that marks every act of coming into the world—demands to be remembered in the abulic being that installs itself in the world after each birth. In the words of Lyotard, childhood is "the event of a possible and radical alteration in the flux that pushes things to repeat the same" (1997: 72). Childhood is a faculty that gives a name to something that "already is" but yet is not "anything", an abjection, a fright that introduces something that cannot be identified into the world of what is. In yet another Lyotardian metaphor, childhood is the name of a miracle, the interruption of the being of things by the entrance of its other—the other of being.

G. Agamben: childhood, experience, history and language

Just to offer some more elements, let's consider some ideas from *Childhood & History*, a text that Giorgio Agamben, Italian translator of W. Benjamin, wrote in the late 1970s (2000/1978), a text where Agamben establishes a fundamental connection between the categories of experience, language, history, and childhood (2000/1978: 17–82).

According to Agamben, childhood and language comply with each other. In childhood, the human being constitutes itself as a subject in and by language (2000/1978: 59). Insofar as human beings do not come to the world already speaking, childhood is absence and the search for language; and it is in childhood where we find that discontinuity specifically humane, where it produces the passage from language to words (Saussure), from semiotics to semantics (Benveniste) or the system of signs to discourse. It is in childhood where each human being appropriates language and makes out of the acquired system of signs a discourse with a meaning; that is, it is constituted as a subject of language when saying "I". Childhood, lacking of language, is also its condition of emergency. Perhaps, it is not too much to clarify that we are not thinking of a centered, self-controlled subject who appropriates language like someone who takes a fish out of the sea, but about a subjectivity that it is constituted and that constitutes itself in the interior of complex discursive and non-discursive practices—like education or philosophy—that go through it.

At the same time, it is in this discontinuity between what is linguistic and what is human, between semiotics and semantics, that Agamben finds the historicity of the human being (2000/1978: 67). If a human being is a historical being, it is because he has a childhood, because language is not given "by nature", but because he has to learn to speak (since the moment he is born), because he hasn't been born already speaking, but because he talks and he is talked about submerging within a history. If there is no possibility for a human being to be a-historic, it is precisely because he does not speak since "ever", because he has to learn to speak (to speak to itself, to be spoken) in a childhood that cannot be universalized or anticipated.

On the other hand, childhood adheres to experience also. Experience is the difference between what is linguistic and what is human, between what is given and what is learnt, between what we have and what we do not have when we are born. Thus, that human beings are not born speaking already, that they have a childhood, that their way of speaking and being spoken is not determined beforehand, is what constitutes an experience (2000/1978: 65). Therefore, in experience, in childhood as experience, a human being constitutes itself as a historical being.

It is not only about a chronological matter. Experience and childhood do not simply precede language and stop existing once the human being gains access to words (2000/1978: 62), or it is accessed by it. Agamben comes to attest (2000/1978: 68) that one and the other are original, founding, transcendental conditions because there is no humanity (the condition of being human) without them, there is no subject that can speak (nor be spoken to) without them. In a sense, we are always learning how to speak (and how to be spoken to), we never "know" how to speak (nor we are all "known" by language) in a definite form, our experience never ends in language. When we believe that we know it all, we have become nature. Without the experience of childhood, we are inert nature, a normality that cannot be modified, but not a historicity that can always be modified. In this case, experience and childhood (childhood experience, the childhood of experience) are conditions of possibilities of human existence, no matter its age.

Agamben writes,

> It is because of this that the history of humanity cannot be a continuous progress of humanity that speaks, throughout a linear continuity; in its essence, history is an interval, discontinuity, an *epoche*. What has childhood as homeland and origin must proceed its path through childhood and in childhood.
>
> (2000/1978: 68)

Because there is childhood (and birth) human history cannot be continuous, lineal, and natural. That the human history has a childhood for its homeland means that it is originated from it, and without it, it is nothing. Without childhood (and experience) there is no human history, nor experience, nor language, nor humanity. With childhood (and experience) human history, language, and humanity becomes possible.

What the three conceptions of childhood that I have just sketched have in common is that for all of them, childhood is something that inherently constitutes human life, and therefore could never be abandoned, forgotten or overcome. In this way, they refuse to go along with the idea of the transformation of childhood into adulthood as a primary pedagogical project, and introduce the need to think of another relation between childhood and education. Beyond the ideal of child-formation, education might be what fosters, nurtures and cares for the experience of childhood itself—what helps us not to forget childhood, but rather to, in Lyotard's words, preserve *infantia* in infancy, or, in Deleuze's, to encounter becoming-child, or, in Agamben's terms, to relate to childhood as experience.

In this record, childhood has stopped being a moment, a chronological stage, and it has become a condition of possibilities of a certain human existence. Far from being a stage that has to be overcome, it becomes a situation to be established, taken care of, and nurtured. It happens that in our contemporary societies there is little space for experience or, better yet, experience has become a mask "inexpressive, impenetrable, always the same" (Benjamin, 1989/1913: 41) of the adult, the one "what are you going to do about it; this is how things are; always have been and always will be", the one of defeat, resignation, and determinism. Experience goes from being a simulation of a life not lived, of dreams not accomplished, not even attempted; the spear of an adult that fights his own childhood, that one that does not forget its dreams. Our times are hostile to childhood and that simulation of experience is one of its preferred weapons. But we are thinking about another experience, the mask of uncomfortable dreams, indispensable yet unrealizable; the one that faces its other mask, it fights, resists, it harasses it; a companion experience of childhood.

The childhood that we affirm is a possibility—not thought of and unforeseeable—of the human existence. It is a chance to open that experience to novelty, to difference; it is a "figure of start" (Larrosa, 2000: 16), in the sense of an image that opens a future, the unexpected, the different, the unsuspected, and unbelievable.

Lyotard suggests making fruitful the occurrence that entails each birth (Lyotard, 1997/1991: 69). Perceived under this light, childhood is the realm of "as if", of "pretend that", of "and if things were different…"; it is to take seriously the novelty of each birth; it is to not let them determine oneself by the most diverse conditionings; it is to impede that this birth empty itself; it is to bet on the fruits that could come out of it; it is to turn multiple and diverse such novelty; it is to prolong the life of the occurrence without it stop being an occurrence, it is to affirm it in the other, it is difference, what in itself does not contain nor reveal.

As the first age (in the temporal sense but also ontological), childhood is the positivity of a multiple progression, a productivity without mediation, the affirmation that there is no predetermined path that a child should follow to become an adult, an immanent exercise of potentials (Katz, 1996: 90).

I offer these alternative notions of childhood, not because they complement each other, nor to prove the force of any given idea of childhood, but on the contrary, in order to avoid the implicit pressure of "reason" to subscribe to one particular, "correct" philosophical theory. In a sense it would be simpler—and probably more articulate—to limit myself to one of these conceptions, but I believe that an open interpretive framework offers more hope for clearing the ground for rethinking the relationship between childhood and education, and the place of philosophy between them. Because I prefer to speak, finally, from my own experience about/as/with childhood, my further remarks in this chapter will be offered within the context of the actual practice of accomplishing philosophical conversations with children—encounters that I have found, almost categorically, to challenge any one theoretical approach.

Thinking the experience of philosophical thinking in the context of Brazilian public schooling

My work in schools and universities in Brazil throughout the past decade and more, during which I and my colleagues have labored to introduce the experience of philosophical thinking in classrooms and other group settings, has led us to question the value of philosophizing within the traditional Platonic ideal of child-formation, or even Lipman's ideal of the formation of the reasonable citizen. Rather, we have sought consciously to promote experiences of philosophical thinking that enable everyone involved in them to *think differently* than the ways we are used to think, and that we are forced or manipulated into thinking by the dominant cultural forces of our time. Our goal has been to establish new relationships within ourselves, with others, to how and what we think, and therefore, to the way we live with ourselves and with the others. We found ourselves driven forward in this search by an experience of cultural dislocation—the outcome of engaging in educational and philosophical work with children and illiterate adults in public schools located in marginalized urban and suburban regions of Rio de Janeiro.[5]

In order to open a space for these new relationships, the three main terms of the concept "experience of philosophical thinking" need to be unpacked, for all three are not only philosophical concepts, but contestable ones as well. Our project has both theoretical and practical aspirations, at the same time that we practice the experiences of philosophical thinking, we encounter this practice with the theoretical discourses of various contemporary philosophers. We do not belong to any of these philosophers, but befriend them, so to speak, in our efforts to found our practice. And indeed we find that the category of "experience", for example, has a long history in various philosophical traditions. Michel Foucault's synthesis, for example, identifies experience as an interactive combination of theory and practice. For him, experience is a kind of theoretical practice or practical theory, in which the dominant idea is that of movement, displacement, and transformation. In effect, a thinking experience is a living, dynamic form, through the process of which we never end in the place we began; nor do we think in the same way that we thought when we entered it.

In this same sense, as we have seen in our Presentation, Foucault (1994)[6] opposes experience and truth as two possibilities of writing. One can write a book under the logic of truth, in which case the author's aim is to transmit a truth he possesses to his readers. If the reader is also guided by the model of truth, he reads in order to learn a truth that he does not yet know. On the other hand, a book written under the logic of experience also affirms truths—there is no way not to do so—but the main sense of writing is not to transmit a truth but to put into question the truth in which the writer is already installed. There could also be readers under the logic of experience who do not read a book to learn what they are ignorant of, but to challenge what they already know— to put their relationship to the truths affirmed in the text into question. Of course there is no final, determined relationship between writing and reading, experience and truth. A book written as experience could be read as truth, and vice versa. And according to Foucault, reading as experience is not only about a possible relationship to what is written, but also to the method employed by the writer. When the guiding methodology follows not truth but experience, even the how and the why of the writer's process are put into question. From the point of view of the writer, this means that, at the beginning of the writing experience, he not only does not know what he will write, but also how he will arrive where he finally arrives.

What Foucault suggests about writing could well be considered as a way of thinking about teaching philosophy. A teacher who relates herself to philosophy as truth may expect her students to learn the philosophical truths she will transmit or mediate in her classes. On the other hand, there may well be philosophy teachers guided by the logic of experience who will also affirm philosophical truths in their classes, but they do not do so in order that their students learn them, but rather in order to problematize the relationship that both—students and teacher—have to the truths in which they are already installed. The difference, then, is that in the first case, the teacher not only knows exactly what to teach, but she is also concerned that her students learn the pathways, instruments and pedagogical strategies that guide and determine her teaching. In the second case, the teacher not only does not want to anticipate what her students will learn, but her pedagogical method—the method, that is, through which she and her students will arrive at questioning their relationship to what they already know and think—will be constructed through the teaching process itself.

In this sense thinking, guided by the logic of experience, puts itself into question—it thinks itself in such a way that it cannot continue to be thought as it was previously thought. Foucault (1984) said it nicely in naming philosophy as a practice (in Greek, *askesis*). What is philosophy as an activity, as an exercise, if it is not "the critical work of thinking about itself, if it does not consist in an attempt to think how and to what extent it would be possible to think differently instead of legitimating what we already know"?

(Foucault, 1984: 15–16). Therein lies the main significance of promoting philosophical experiences with teachers and students—not to legitimate what we or they know, but to foster difference in their thinking and our thinking as well.

Certainly the question "what is philosophy?" is also a controversial one, and the expression "philosophical experience" is not at all clear on its face value. The issue is complex enough to resist resolution in a few pages, but a few observations may at least point to the path we are following. One may, for example, distinguish between two dimensions of philosophy, the process and the product—or, we might say, the verb and the noun. The product is constituted in the powerful discursive constructs of iconic texts, well-established institutions, and preferred methods, built up at least since the pre-Socratics into what is called the Western philosophical tradition. The other dimension could be characterized, with Foucault, more by its effects than its activity, as "a diagnosis of the present" or a "critical ontology of ourselves" (1994: 665, 575). These latter are the results of philosophical experiences: after them, we are in a better condition to understand our times and our place in them. But experience itself has to do mainly with the verb and the process. Foucault appeals to a parallel conceptual framework when he characterizes philosophy as "the movement through which, not without efforts and obstacles, dreams and illusions, we detach ourselves from what is taken as true, and we look for other rules of the game" (1994: 110). That is to say, as experience, philosophy is the movement through which thinking enters a path along which there is no opportunity to return to the point of departure. It entails a kind of radical affectivity, in that our truths and fixed points are disturbed, problematized, questioned. New rules are needed, and a new relation to truth emerges.

Finally, thinking is as controversial a concept as are experience and philosophy. Again, we are faced by another issue with a complex philosophical background. As Foucault was more interested in issues of clear social relevance, like madness, power and sexuality, he did not give specific attention to questions like "What does it mean to think?" or "What is the place of thinking in human life?" Here we might call on G. Deleuze's notion of thinking as encounter, and on his critique of the idea of representation and what he calls the "dogmatic image" of thinking (1968) that has, with few exceptions, pervaded the history of Western philosophy. His critique is inspiring because of its relevance to contemporary prevalent images of thinking, especially among pedagogical discourses. In the Deleuzian sense, to think is not to produce a representation or to experience a recognition of something, but is an encounter with the external signs that call it to our attention. In order to think, a kind of deconstructive movement is first needed, in order to override the traditional image and to, as much as possible, render us sensitive to what is "outside" us. Thinking is not opposed to sensitivity; quite the contrary, it is nurtured by it, it originates in it. Even more, thinking is a passion—immanent, spontaneous, self-caused, and not the result of some external will.

Thus, in this preliminary sense of the term, we might say that our task consists in promoting the experience of philosophical of thinking with others, in institutions such as schools and universities, but certainly not limited to those places. In so doing, we reclaim and recreate a long tradition of philosophical dialogue. We are not particularly interested in teaching or learning the truths affirmed in the history of philosophy, even though we are readers of that history; rather, we try to do what philosophers of that tradition do. In so doing, we encounter "lovers of wisdom" (or those with the "wisdom of lovers". to show the specific form of passion required by practitioners of philosophy)—those looking for something similar to what we are looking for or, to put it differently, those who describe their own philosophical labor in a way close to our own, and who help us clarify and even discover our own. As such, we are engaged in what Pierre Hadot, who strongly influenced Foucault's reading of ancient cultures, called "spiritual exercises" (1993: 19 ff.). As a spiritual exercise, philosophy is a form of living which engages the whole of existence—a life-changing conversion.

The expression "spiritual exercises" is not free of misunderstanding, as Hadot (1993: 20), himself acknowledged,[7] but its chief virtue here is in its evocation of a culture and a discursive framework in which thinking is not understood as just an intellectual action. Foucault built upon Hadot's concept of philosophy as spiritual exercise to affirm that it is only through what he calls the "Cartesian moment" that modern philosophy came to be understood as solely a cognitive exercise (2001: 2–39). In spiritual practice, there is no way of building knowledge or reaching truth that does not involve a transformative practice, or *askesis*, of the self. The notion of self-care is a guiding principle of spiritual practice, and in classical Greek thought is a wide category that includes, among other things, the pursuit of self-knowledge. In modern thought, self-knowledge is understood as no more than a privileged relation to oneself, and thus does not require any transformation of the subject. But in the notion of the experience of philosophical thinking offered here, the entire life is put into question. We are not interested in this or that information or knowledge, in any specific truth; we do not teach techniques in order that students practice intellectual skills, learn how to answer this or that kind of question, or recognize this or that type of fallacy. Rather, we are primarily interested in students and teachers entering a zone of interrogation—in putting themselves, their lives, their passions and beliefs into question through the experience of thinking together.

Within the context of a culture of self-care, some ancient thinkers developed spiritual exercises that are suggestive for the project of the experience of philosophical thinking. Philo of Alexandria left two lists of exercises that include such practices as: thorough investigation (*skepsis*), reading (*anagnosis*), listening (*akroasis*), attention (*prosoche*) and meditation (*meletai*)[8]. These are more than exercises in piety; rather, they seek to cultivate a way of seeing and being in the world. As activities, they hardly entail the transmission of pre-determined knowledge from one person to another; nor are they examples of a totalizing technique, or a formula which guarantees that the one practicing them will thereby achieve epistemological certainty and existential security. Rather the philosophical experience cultivated by these exercises is an individual and, at the same time, shared journey of inquiry, discovery and transformation— one that calls upon us to think, not just about living, but about the way we ourselves live.

The experience of philosophical thinking is then, first and most importantly a matter of sensitivity. Rather than a form of knowledge or wisdom, it is a *practical relationship* to knowledge or wisdom. We live in the epoch of the "knowledge society", in which information is in fact mistaken for knowledge, and every "citizen" is endlessly encouraged to "have his own opinion". Of course it is important that the poor and the dispossessed, those who have been silenced for centuries, embrace their fundamental right to speak and to express themselves. But if we are really interested in their speaking in their own voices, and not in the voices of the ventriloquists of popular culture, the corporate media, the political, academic or therapeutic elites, or, even more directly, in the voices of market or capital, the issue of enabling the voices of the marginalized becomes more complicated. Why would it be so important that everyone express their "own" opinion if, in the end, very similar opinions are expressed? We can, in fact, make a distinction between "voice" and "opinion". One's own voice emerges, I would suggest, only after a conversion of sorts, which, in the case of the oppressed, involves a recognition and repudiation of the alienating cultural processes to which they have been subjected, and before which they have been rendered epistemologically, politically and pedagogically passive. Otherwise, we risk repeating the dialectic of the oppressor and the oppressed, with the positions slightly shifted to present a media-managed simulacrum of the "liberation" suggested by having "a right to one's own opinion". What is needed is a process of locating and working to deconstruct the deeper structures that disable their own active thinking. What liberation is to be found in any pedagogical practice whose operative metaphor is "filling", whether from the outside or the inside? What is necessary is to create educational conditions for thinking *with* others in thoughtful and meaningful ways, under the radar of the hugely influential media totality of our time.

Philosophical experience does not "fill" interlocutors with dogmas, assumptions, and beliefs, nor even with interesting ideas, concepts or questions. Rather, it "empties" the interlocutors of unexamined ideas, dogmas, beliefs, questions and values. The contemporary Brazilian poet Manoel de Barros (2000: 9) expresses this idea succinctly: "Unlearning eight hours a day teaches the principles [of]... a didactics of invention". There are so many things to unlearn in order to create conditions for learning differently: unlearn the relationship to thinking fostered by educational institutions; unlearn the way we think about our students. Unlearn, unlearn and unlearn, this is our lemma. Above all, unlearn a way of learning that inhibits experience. If this is true of students who need to recreate conditions in order to think powerfully, it is even more true of teachers whose calling it is to help others to learn to think.

In our practice with teachers and adult students, the project of unlearning is also supported by another spiritual exercise—"becoming a child". In his book *Exercises on Being a Child* (*Exercícios de ser criança*, 1999) the same Manoel de Barros speaks for what we can learn from practicing a childlike way of being in the world. Children, he argues, are less "full", "fresher", less prejudiced, more open to putting themselves freely into question. Because of their briefer exposure to oppressive institutions, they are closer to that state in which they can really think for themselves. In our philosophical exercises, teachers learn from their students to "become a child" by participating in activities such as painting, drawing, and formulating questions as a child does them. It is not a matter of imitating a child or of behaving "childishly", but of facing our own lives as children are used to doing—as if we were doing something for the first time, as if anything were possible. More than once, teachers have told us that through these kinds of experiences, they realize that they have never truly done what they appeared to be doing every day, not only to themselves but also to others. As such, teachers who teach in a childlike way teach as if they have never really taught before, as if they were finding a new beginning for a different practice under the same name.

The prospects for promoting philosophical experience in the great majority of public schools in Brazil are buffeted by contradictory forces. On the one hand, institutional culture and practice seem completely hostile to the experience of philosophical thinking as described above. In effect, they offer disciplinary conditions so adverse that the very possibility of such experiences appears to be a quixotic fantasy. The bureaucratization of the labor of teaching, the technification of human relations within the system, and the outsized social demand for "productivity" made upon schools in general appear to offer no space for experience. More, the reifying force of culture imprisons everyone in the illusion that everything seems already to have been thought; any kind of problematization or questioning process seems useless or meaningless, like beating the ocean with a broom. On the other hand, the sensed necessity for transformation—the frustration with a clearly dysfunctional status quo—is equally powerful in those same institutions. And it is in the gaps that sometimes become apparent in this contradictory context that real opportunities for philosophical practice emerge. Wherever we find indications of an open disposition towards and interest in philosophy, we accept the challenge and enter the situation, offering the experience of philosophical thinking to children and teachers in the form of spiritual exercises, in the context of their ordinary practice. We gamble on the force of experience even in adverse contexts, in which there seem to be no conditions for thinking. We play the pedagogical game we are given in a way that suggests changing its rules; we act as if experience and thinking were possible, even if they are not. We do not, as in traditional utopian thinking, move from the real to the possible, but we consider the impossible real, always in expectation of the new—that something interesting might happen.

What is philosophical education about?
Two pedagogical paragons

I would like to return to a reflection on the pedagogical assumptions of the practice I am describing in the context of two other philosophers who have provided it with the most inspiration. Again, to call upon a variety of philosophical sources is not intended to affirm any new official heterodoxy, but rather to reinforce a spectrum of theoretical possibility, and to suggest a creative interplay between theory and practice.

Socrates first, of course, but not the Socrates who is usually invoked—the champion, that is, of dialogue, the master of *maieusis*, who brings to term in students what they are already pregnant with. Rather, I would like to focus on an argument that Socrates offers in the *Apology*. In defending himself against the accusation of corrupting the young, he claims never to have been a teacher of anyone (Plato, *Apology of Socrates,* 33a–c); and yet a little further along, he affirms that if he is killed, his death will be useless because "those who have learned with me" will continue doing what he does (33a–c; 39c–d). Socrates affirms, then, a sort of pedagogical scandal: the idea of a pedagogical situation in which the student learns without a teacher. What Socrates helps us to think here is that there is no necessary causality, nor even directionality, between teacher and learner, or the acts of teaching and learning. Someone does not teach but others learn with him. Someone learns but does not learn what he learns from someone who teaches it. What Socrates helps us to question is the pedagogical dogma that what a student learns is in the teacher, and is somehow transmitted to, or made to appear, in the learner through a certain behavior or even a disposition of the teacher.

This Socratic act of deconstruction would appear to emancipate and empower both the learning and teaching processes. But the French contemporary philosopher Jacques Rancière has questioned the political dimension of this position. According to him (1987), Socrates lies: it is not true that he teaches nothing; in fact he does teach, and what he teaches is, specifically, a relationship to knowledge from a position of superiority, which he legitimates through the mythic tale of the Delphic oracle. On this account, he proves his reputation as the wisest man in Athens through searching everywhere for a wiser, and discovering that his superior wisdom consists in the fact that he recognizes the small value of his knowledge, whereas no one else does.[9] On the account of Rancière (1987)—whose philosophical approach has very few elements in common with Deleuze, Lyotard and Foucault—Socrates is in fact claiming superiority through imposing his view of the "best" relation to knowledge on others, and thereby teaching what an emancipator would never teach—the distance between the teacher and the student in relation to knowledge. After conversing with Socrates, all his interlocutors know how much further they are than him from the appropriate relationship to knowledge. Even though he does not teach any knowledge content, he does teach that everyone who seeks a proper relationship to knowledge should have a

Socratic one. This position cannot but place the learner in an inferior position to the teacher.

Contrary to this position of implicit superiority, Rancière considers that affirming the *opinion* that all intelligences are equal is the single most important condition of intellectual emancipation (1987: 77). Rancière opposes opinion to truth. Whereas the latter can be demonstrated, justified, and leads to certainty, the former gives space to *un*certain experiences that will seek to verify it (ibid.: 78). If the pedagogical principle that all intelligences are equal is expressed as an opinion and not a truth, it also means that its value is more political than epistemological. In this view, what differentiates emancipatory from "stultification" pedagogical practices is the relationship to intelligence (and knowledge) and to the will that each establishes. A stultifying teacher liberates the will of the student, but yokes the intelligence of the learner to the intelligence of the teacher. On the contrary, the emancipatory teacher works upon the will of the student through liberating her intelligence to work by itself—which he can do only under the presupposition that all intelligences are equal. This is why Socrates does not emancipate, since he presupposes an unequal ratio of intelligence between himself and his interlocutors.

Although I am sensitive to this critique, I find both Rancière's *and* Socrates' positions inspiring. In spite of their political disagreement, their emancipatory teachers have something in common. Even though we are less sure of how Socrates relates to ignorance than how Rancière does, they both affirm the position of ignorance, and both profess ignorance of what the other learns with them. Both want their students to learn a specific relationship to knowledge, although those relationships are very different. Socrates wants others to know that the most important relation to knowledge is in the realization of one's ignorance. That is why he deconstructs what others think they know. Rancière wants others to experience the equality of intelligences. As such, we can combine Socrates and Rancière in a pedagogical practice that encounters the other in order to deconstruct her knowledge under the presupposition of the equality of intelligence. We do not need to assume any specific relationship between knowledge and ignorance in order to affirm the value of a pedagogical practice based on deconstruction of what we already know or think. Like Socrates *and* Rancière, we can operate on the salutary assumption that there is no causal relationship between teaching and learning. We teach without knowing what a student is learning, or even if she is in fact learning anything. We do not know and we do not want to know or anticipate what a student may be learning—whether it be something she already knows, or simply the knowledge of her ignorance. Rather, we work to establish a context for thinking, and a pedagogical relationship in which the student realizes that the teacher does not want to transfer, bestow, or engineer the appearance of anything to or in the student, but is confident in the potential of her thinking, and in her capacity to share a thinking process with others.

Philosophical experience and the childhood of education: some final examples

At the moment, several valued colleagues and myself are developing experiences in philosophical thinking for a project called "Em Caxias a filosofia en-caixa?"[10] in two public schools with socio-economically depressed populations in the suburbs of Rio de Janeiro. The project is sponsored by the Center for Philosophical Studies of Childhood at the State University of Rio de Janeiro. I will finish by offering a few examples of thinking encounters that have already taken place there, in hopes that they may suggest a different form of living the relationship between childhood, philosophy and education. One of them took place at the university itself. From time to time we bring a class of students there, so that they can become familiar with a territory that is very far both from their lives and from their own imagination.[11] Once there, we do a philosophical session together, in a classroom that we have furnished with comfortable chairs and pillows, lots of books, games, toys and DVDs.

Last year, something interesting happened on one of these visits. The children—ranging in age from nine to thirteen years old (ages are neither regular nor homogeneous in these classes)—were entering the main building to take the elevators to the twelfth floor, where the classroom is located. It was a strange environment for them. The building is huge, aggressively functional, all grey concrete slabs and pillars, pylons, and exposed utilities, drawing the eye along its sweeping interior vistas. It is a building more or less reserved for adults, and this group of more than 20 young students suggested an odd invasion to this uniform place. When we had entered one of the large elevators, the operator, surprised by the children's sudden appearance there, asked them if they were visiting the university. Nearly at the same moment, a number of them answered loudly, their voices ringing clear and strong, "No, we are here to do philosophy!" The operator laughed, as did the other adults on the elevator.

This may seem to be a trivial anecdote, but if we imagine substituting these children with a group of philosophy students on their way to the ninth floor to attend their classes in the history of philosophy, and imagine the operator asking the same question, one wonders if they might have answered that in fact they were there to learn and not to do philosophy. It may be argued that the aim of academic philosophy as taught at the university is not to do philosophy but to learn it as a condition for doing it later, but the usual fact of the matter is that, in "learning" it, students tend to form a kind of relationship to philosophy that infinitely postpones their doing it, and in some cases actually prevents it. As Rancière would put it, what they learn is that they are inferior to the philosophers whom they are studying, and dependent on them for any knowledge they acquire. They are taught in such a way that renders it difficult or impossible to see themselves as active subjects of philosophical thinking. The moment of actually doing philosophy will never arise in the context of this relationship to the discipline.

The children, on the other hand, have learned another relationship to philosophy through their experiences of thinking, and they see themselves as active participants in the enterprise. They understand themselves as doing what philosophers do, and thus they see themselves as philosophers. Many will question whether what they are doing is actually philosophy at all. I for one am not sure. How could we be sure without first staking a contestable cultural/historical claim on a given definition of philosophy? Wouldn't we need to ask the students themselves about their own conception of philosophy before we could consider that question? In any case, even if they are not doing philosophy, some meaningful learning may emerge in their acting *as if* they were doing philosophy. Moreover, these young people made it clear from the outset that they were not just "visiting" a university—in fact their remark implies that they understood themselves as being there in order to do just what one is expected to do in that sort of a place. They affirmed that they were not just second-category visitors—that they had every right to do what is supposed to be done there, a right that trumps age or social position. This represents not philosophical but political learning: they have discovered and affirmed a primary public space for thinking, and claimed the common right to participate actively in that space with others like them. As such, these students showed that what they had learned about philosophy in school—the specific relationship to thinking that is practiced in the experiences we offered them—is in no way restricted to school. Their understanding of the enterprise is simple, clear, and direct, and they take the practice absolutely seriously— they understand it implicitly as a way of thinking that results in significant personal development of the one who practices it. This is what these students learn: in fact, they do not learn philosophy; rather they learn to build a relationship to philosophy through thinking with others. Meanwhile, what this experience with philosophy—this active relationship to thinking—may bring forth in them is something that we cannot and should not anticipate, lest we fall back into the illusion that we have "taught them something".

Speaking with the head

The second example I want to offer comes from another group of students from the same school, this time in their own classroom in their worn and threadbare school in the suburbs. We were discussing the meaning and significance of doing philosophy, in a classroom that we had equipped specifically for our sessions. Like the one at the university, we have removed the hard benches, painted the walls with bright colors, and put in some lighter and softer furniture. The students and teachers from this school call this space the "thinking classroom" ("Sala do pensamento"). So, when we asked our students what they thought about their experience with philosophy so far—if they had learned anything from it and if so what, and what kinds of effects they found in themselves as a result of this practice—they began offering ideas and examples.

One of them—I shall call him Vinicius—spoke about some of the different things he could now do that he could not before. In fact, they did not sound particularly unique; but he finished his intervention with a remark that commanded our attention. He said, "Before philosophy I spoke with my mouth; since I have been doing philosophy I speak with my head".

The image stuck us immediately as significant, but we did not pursue it in the conversation, or even attempt to develop a hermeneutical path in order to determine the exact meaning of his intervention. In fact, he may have intended to say something that we did not understand him to be saying, or vice versa; but to inscribe what children say in the grid of our own adult hermeneutical devices is perhaps not that interesting after all. Depending on our presuppositions and theoretical lenses and frameworks, a number of possible interpretations may emerge, but it might be more interesting to listen to this voice from the standpoint of our own experience, even though the resulting interpretation may not necessarily correspond at all to what Vinicius was "actually" saying. In other words, instead of proposing and defending an interpretation of what he said, I want to draw some implications from it for my own thinking about our practice. As such, they are childlike words that will be read in a childlike way.

The first idea inspired by Vinicius's words is that whatever he understands by "the mouth" and "the head", the former expresses a kind of being which is in a relation of part to whole with the latter. The mouth is a part of the head, and there are lots of other parts in a head besides the mouth. This signifies to me that if, before his philosophical experience, he spoke only with his mouth, and since then speaks with his whole head, he has more options for speaking now than he had before.

Second, we do in fact speak with our mouths, but we do not literally or specifically speak with our heads, even though our mouths are located in our heads. In effect, we can say that we speak with our heads only in an indirect or metaphorical way. This capacity for indirect or metaphorical speech suggests that through the experience of philosophy he learned to explore another dimension of language than the one he was accustomed to. Before his experience with philosophy, "speaking" belonged to one semantic register, and "head" to another. After philosophy, he could calmly put these two registers together, in his thinking and in his speech. He learned that he could use the words not only to say what they are "supposed" to say (and therefore to think only what "ought" to be thought) but in a second order way. He learned to think and speak in a broader dimension than the one we are used to in everyday language.

Third, the expansive image—that is, from part to whole—employed by Vinicius is interesting, not only because it expresses an enlargement and complexification of his capacity for speaking and thinking, but it also signals a movement from an ordinary and naturalized relationship to what it is supposed to be thought and spoken, to an extraordinary and unnatural form of relationship. In effect, it is not a natural thing to say—we are not supposed to be speaking with our heads, but with our mouths. His image represents a kind of desacralization of the function of both head and mouth; it is in fact illogical to move the speaking function from the mouth to the head. As such, Vinicius expresses a kind of salutary indiscipline in his thinking through philosophy; through our thinking experiences he learned to deconstruct the framework that disciplined the way he thought and spoke about his own thinking and speaking. What seemed unnatural before philosophy now was seen as a conquest.

These are just a few examples of a more extended practice. My own strong impression is that, through the philosophical experiences of thinking we have offered, these groups of young people have begun to attach much more value, care and attention to what they say and think than before they began seeing themselves as doing what philosophers do. And they share this process with their other teachers, who also take part in this enlargement of the possibilities of speaking and thinking. Coincidently, they find more sense and meaning in the experience of school itself.

Some ideas

The primary aim of this chapter has been to explore how the relationships between philosophy and childhood could be thought and practiced from a perspective other than the traditional one, which I have traced to Plato. In this sense, I have tried to offer conceptual elements towards a reterritorialization of the relationship between childhood and philosophy, to put it in Deleuzian terms. These elements include some diverse philosophical approaches to childhood and to the practice of philosophical thinking, as well as some concrete examples from my own practice. It has not been my intention to build a set of claims about the relations I am exploring, nor to found an educational model—which, although it may have been a tactical necessity in order to introduce philosophy into childhood education a few decades ago, is no longer that productive. And in order to maintain a fluid and emergent relation between theory and practice, I have called on a rather extended number of authors and categories, whose ideas act to deconstruct both traditional views of childhood and implicitly, of the education of childhood.

My colleagues and I have never been very sure of how to justify the name "philosophy" in this enterprise, undertaken in a social and pedagogical zone that, in many ways, could not be further from the familiar terrain of philosophy as understood in the academy. Nor is the difficulty here an issue of class: it would probably be easier to bring philosophy as academically understood to the more privileged zones of the upper middle class private school, but probably even harder to bring it as an experience of transformative thinking. An institutionalized context pushing so obdurately in other directions makes us question not only how to do philosophy in such a setting, but whether it is possible at all depending on the way we understand philosophy. It seems most probable that a "childhood of education"—that new beginning so relentlessly invoked by the new understanding of the relationship between the child and time that I have sketched above—implicitly entails a "childhood of school". In its present form, the school is actually hostile to the form of childhood that we seek to foster and care for. It must find itself in a new relationship to childhood before philosophy, as an experience of transformative thinking, can really be practiced in it. But the schools we find are the ones we have, and the lack of meaning that we observe there cries out to us, and compels us to enter them. We do so *as if* it were possible to establish a new educational relationship to childhood there, and work fully expecting an emergence that cannot be predicted, but that fills us with the energy to continue thinking a new location for the practice of philosophy in the education of childhood. Through what we call philosophy, children of all ages are opening to an ageless childhood in their thinking experience and in their lives. The energies generated by the encounter between childhood and philosophy are unpredictable, and oblige us to pay close attention to what might emerge from it, all the while expecting the unexpectable (as Heraclitus says in his fragment 18) and unlearning the learned, on the assumption that another world is not only possible, but is in fact already present in the way we are living our lives.

Notes

1 All translations in this chapter, whether from Greek, Spanish, French or Portuguese, are the author's unless otherwise specified.
2 For the following, see *Pourparlers* (Paris: Editions Minuit, 1990), Chap. V: "Politique: 16. Contrôle et devenir".
3 For the following, cf. G. Deleuze and F. Guattari, 1980, "10. 1730 – Devenir-intense, devenir.-animal, devenir-imperceptible", pp. 285 ss.
4 All references in this section from Chapter 5, "Survivant. Arendt", are quoted from the Spanish Translation (Lyotard, 1997).
5 This specific project began in 2007. For a detailed description of a one-year experience with adults in these settings, see Kohan and Wozniak, 2010.
6 See for example, "Entretien avec Michel Foucault" (by D. Trombadori) in Foucault (1994), pp. 41–95.
7 The word "spiritual" is full of metaphysical and theological connotations, but the other expressions discussed—and ultimately rejected—by Hadot seem to present other problems. He considers the term "thinking" or "intellectual" exercises, but affirms that both terms seem to leave aside a fundamental dimension of "spiritual exercises": imagination and sensibility. Other expressions he considers are "ethical" and "psychological" exercises, but both are too limiting in that they do not denote the transformation of the world view and of the personality of the person involved in this practice.
8 For the complete list, see Hadot (1993) p. 25 ff.
9 The issue is certainly more complex in the three conversations he describes in *Apology* 21b-23d, but this simplification seems enough for the present argument.
10 In English: "Does Philosophy fit in Caxias? *A Public School Gambles on Thinking*". The original Portuguese, "Em Caxias a Filosofia En-caixa?!", plays with the word "Caxias" which is a name of a city close to Rio de Janeiro, but also signifies "fit". Website in Portuguese: www.filoeduc.org/caxias
11 Most of these students don't even consider the possibility of entering a University in the future. No one has done that in their families, and completing elementary school is considered a great achievement.

Bibliography

Agamben, G. (2000/1978) *Enfance et historie*. Paris: Payot & Rivages.

Aristotle (2003) *The Complete Works of Aristotle*. J. Barnes (ed.). Princeton: Princeton University Press.

Barros, M. de (1999) *Exercícios de ser criança*. Rio de Janeiro: Salamandra.

———. (2000) *O livro das ignoráças*. São Paulo: Record.

Benjamin, W. (1989/1913) "Experiencia", in *Escritos. La literatura infantil, los niños y los jóvenes*. Buenos Aires: Nueva Visión, pp. 41–3.

Deleuze, G. (1968) *Différence et répétition*. Paris: PUF.

———. (1990) *Pourparlers*. Paris: Les Editions de Minuit.

Deleuze, G. and Guattari, F. (1980) *Mille Plateaux. Capitalisme et schizophrénie*. Paris: Les Editions de Minuit.

———. (1991) *Qu'est-ce que la philosophie?* Paris: Les Editions du Minuit.

Foucault, M. (1984) *Histoire de la sexualité*. Paris: Gallimard, t. II: *L'usage des plaisirs*.

———. (1994) *Dits et écrits*. Paris: Gallimard. t. IV.

———. (2001) *L'herméneutique du sujet*. Paris: Gallimard-Seuil

Hadot, P. (1993) *Exercices spirituels et philosophie antique*. Paris: Albin Michel.

Heraclitus (2001) *Heraclitus*. Miroslav Marcovich (ed.). Sankt Augustin: Academia Verlag.

Katz, Ch. S. (1996). Crianceira. O que é a criança. *Cadernos de Subjetividade*. São Paulo: PUC, pp. 90–6.

Kohan, W. and Wozniak, J. (2010) "Philosophy as Spiritual Exercise in an Adult Literacy Course", *Thinking: The Journal of Philosophy for Children*, vol. 19, no. 4, pp. 17–23.

Larrosa, J. (2000) 'Filosofia e infância', *Novedades Educativas*. Buenos Aires, 12, no. 115, July 2000, pp. 16–17.

Liddell, H. and Scott, R. (1966) *A Greek English Lexicon*. Oxford: Clarendon Press.

Lipman, M. (1988) *Philosophy Goes to School*. Philadelphia: Temple University Press.

———. (1998) 'The Contributions of Philosophy to Deliberative Democracy', in D. Evans and I. Kuçuradi (eds) *Teaching Philosophy on the Eve of the Twenty-first Century*. Ankara: International Federation of Philosophical Societies, pp. 6–29.

Lyotard, J.-F. (1997) *Lecturas de infancia*. Buenos Aires: EUDEBA.

Plato (1990) *Platonis Opera* (ed. John Burnet). Oxford: Oxford University Press. Trad. English. *The Dialogues of Plato* (Trans. B. Jowett). New York: Oxford University Press (1989).

Rancière, J. (1987) *Le maître ignorant*. Paris: Fayard.

6 Plato and Socrates

From educator of childhood to childlike educator?

To think is often an opportunity for encounters. To think about childhood presents the opportunity to find out who we are, and to open ourselves to other ways of being. Note that I say, "who we *are*" and not "who we *were*" because childhood is ever present. To think about childhood is also a chance to question what we have constructed in the name of childhood, particularly in education. This is the aim of this chapter. In a sense, this a Foucauldian path and my main aim is to offer some ideas on thinking differently about the place of childhood in education, and, more specifically, the meaning given to philosophy in the education of childhood.

I draw on two ancient Greek philosophers—significant sources in helping me to think about childhood as educating. They are Socrates and Plato, whose relationship, according to contemporary French philosopher Jacques Derrida, constitute philosophy itself (1980: 56). Socrates is the inventor of philosophy as a form of questioning practice; Plato is one of his disciples through whom we know Socrates as the philosopher who wrote nothing down. Plato wrote *dialogues* in which Socrates is the main character. Plato himself (as narrative character) appears in only two of his *dialogues*, which include very different, sometimes contradictory, versions of "Socrates" taking different roles and positions. It is impossible to separate the two figures, but it is also impossible not to try to deal with the hermeneutic dilemma posed by Plato: how can they be separated from each other?

Plato's Socrates is such a powerful figure, that nearly everyone in philosophy has to face him eventually. In this chapter, I refer to many of Plato's *dialogues*, especially the *Phaedrus*, but also *Symposium*, *Theaetetus*, *Charmides*, *Apology*, *Meno* and *Gorgias*. The reasons for this are the inspiring value of these two figures: Plato and Socrates; the central place that Platonic ideas still play in 'Western' Philosophy and Education; and the richness of the Socratic figure in thinking about childhood and its relation to philosophy and education. I do not want to enter the complex hermeneutic problems, nor do I approach them with the pretention of revealing their truth, but rather as inspiring sources of thought about the particular problem I am engaged with here.

In the first part of the chapter, I highlight the way in which philosophy is presented indirectly in some of Plato's *dialogues*, beginning with a characterization that Socrates the philosopher makes of himself in conversation with Phaedrus, drawing in particular on the dialogue with the same name. Thus I invite the reader to think about learning through a philosophical life, as understood by Socrates. The second part details Plato's condemnation of writing in the *Phaedrus*, drawing on the critiques by Derrida and Gilles Deleuze to establish what is at stake in this condemnation. In the third part, I review the pedagogical and political implications of this condemnation and show how it places Plato in a surprising position in relation to his own teacher, Socrates. I present the value of childhood as *pharmakon*[1], with testimonies from various *dialogues*. Finally, through a comparison between childhood and philosophy, I question the educational value of putting childhood and philosophy together. What matters most is not philosophers, but the place given to childhood when the child is educated in the name of philosophy. In other words, what image, concept and place does philosophy give to childhood, while thinking about its education?

I offer a way of writing about childhood that I hope inspires thinking about childlike encounters with childhood. I intend to make space for any childhood educator who is, for example, teaching literacy, to allow herself to become child in the act of reading. This might encourage the move from educator of childhood to childlike educator, a childhood educating.

The presentation of the philosopher

The dialogue *Phaedrus* presents the character Socrates, and an infinite puzzle—that of philosophy; how to live a philosophical life, how and why others can live this life? The puzzle is also that we find Socrates, but not Plato. Plato does not write about himself. His absence is not accidental. As mentioned earlier, he is referred to only a couple of times in the *dialogues*. This absence has a crucial impact on philosophy. The teacher, Socrates, the first to inscribe philosophy as an exercise of words with others in the *polis*[2], does not write himself. The disciple, Plato, writes, but hides behind the narrative character of his teacher. There is no way of having direct contact with Socrates or Plato. To reach Socrates, we must go "through" Plato; to reach Plato, we must go "through" Socrates.

This puzzle also raises questions for students of philosophy. How does one learn to think? What kind of relationship should be established with the teacher? What does one learn? The teacher (Socrates) teaches without writing and condemns writing. His disobedient disciple (Plato) writes in his absence. This is philosophy; an indecipherable repetition and difference[3].

We open the book *Phaedrus*, and already, we find this puzzle of philosophy; thinking that is elaborated and re-elaborated to infinity, a perennial mystery, that of thinking itself in dialogue with itself, impossible to elucidate but at the same time impossible to deceive. We find a virtuality that demands to be unfolded, updated and extended in the most diverse dimensions, endless, irresolvable and crazy. This is also the enigma of the philosophy born of Socrates/Plato. The act of philosophizing carries everywhere and always the contradictory nature of the *pharmakon* in itself. Let me unpack this statement.

In the *Phaedrus*, Socrates meets Phaedrus, who carries with him a *pharmakon*; a papyrus speech under his cloak. Socrates follows Phaedrus, and they look for the best place to hear this *pharmakon*, that is, Lysias' written speech.

Lysias, the most skilled speech writer among the Athenians, writes about love (*erotikos*) in a way that Phaedrus does not feel himself capable of explaining. The topic is significant: love is one of the few, if not the only forms of knowledge, which Socrates claims to know about in the dialogues ("nothing different than things concerning love I admit knowing" (*ouden phemi allo epistasthai e ta erotika, Banquete* 177d)). He learned what he knows about love from a woman, a priestess, a foreigner, Diotima of Mantinea (ibid., 201d). The sources of this knowledge are external, in two senses. The knowledge of a philosopher is not knowledge of content, or possession, but knowledge of relationship, affection and passion.

Lysias writes a speech about the only knowledge which the philosopher admits knowing, the knowledge that leads him to madness. That is the strength of the *pharmakon*. Facing the *pharmakon,* Socrates is himself lost: he wants only to hear it. Thus begins the philosopher: examining claims to knowledge about love, knowledge of relationships, sensation, passion, a meeting with other bodies and other souls. The kind of knowledge nobody who lives a philosophical life can do without. A philosopher's search begins with hope, knowledge and a path to be taken with that which is most vital, and at the same time, putting life in question, as *eros* does with Socrates.

Socrates expresses his knowledge of Phaedrus in such an intimate way that not knowing Phaedrus would also mean not knowing himself (*Phaedrus* 228a). This is no small detail for someone like Socrates who is obsessively concerned with knowing himself. The relationship between knowledge and forgetting oneself also appears strongly at a crucial moment in the beginning of the *Apology* (17a). With his life at stake, and after hearing the charges against him, Socrates says the accusers were so convincing, that even though they were far from the truth, they almost managed to make him forget himself. The "almost" marks the risk of a death more vital for the philosopher than the one that could result from the trial.

Socrates knows Phaedrus. Phaedrus also knows Socrates, to the point of using similar words (236c) to Socrates soon after reading Lysias' speech. Philosophy is a conversation among friends.

In the beginning of the *Phaedrus* all the conditions for philosophizing are not given. There are others, including several external factors—the outside temperature and that of the body, the air we breathe, the tranquility of the environment that would allow us to be uninterrupted, pleasant sounds, calm music perhaps, etc. Most important is time. There must be enough time to philosophize—free time, *schole*, the kind that can not be measured by clocks and watches; infinite time, without pressure, shared time, time of friendship, time of childhood and time of truth, without conditions, apart from those of the conversation itself. Phaedrus and Socrates have this time available and they also find an appropriate place to talk.

Maybe some implications for the theme of childhood as educating can be anticipated at this point. All these conditions for philosophizing seem more childlike than adultlike. Let's focus on time: *chronos* and *aion* are two Greek words denoting time. The former designates the "number of movements according to before-after relationships" (Aristotle, *Physics*, IV 11, 219b); the latter "a child playing a game of oppositions; the realm of a child" (Heraclitus, fr. 52). Adult experience of time is highly chronological, adults need to measure and order time, to organize and plan their lives in terms of the consecutive succession of movements that conform to time as *chronos*. In contrast, children seem more sensitive to a qualitative, *aionic* experience of time. Play does not fit in well with *chronos*. In this sense, children seem closer to the time condition for philosophy than adults. Children could teach adults to unlearn their present chronological experience of time and relearn an *aionic* one, at least in order to do philosophy.

Once the conditions of the conversation are established, philosophizing begins with knowledge about oneself. Socrates affirms his paradoxical position. He shows himself incapable of knowing himself, only a few lines after having stated that not knowing Phaedrus would imply forgetting himself. But how is it possible to forget that which is unknown? It is only possible for someone as close to *pharmakon* as Socrates. He seems to deal with conflicting demands: on the one hand, if he admits knowing himself then he would not be able to devote his life to investigating himself, as is confirmed in the *Phaedrus* (and many other *dialogues*), because why would he research what he already knows? On the other hand, neither can he devote himself to this life, if he does not know himself, for it is this knowledge which justifies and gives meaning to a life of searching for himself.

Thus Socrates appears embarrassed: knowing himself and not knowing himself are both impossible and necessary—like the *pharmakon*, like philosophy in the *polis*, like the only life that makes sense to Socrates, that which carries him to death. Perhaps this is why Phaedrus describes Socrates as the most extraordinary of all Athenians, without a place and unfamiliar (*atopotatos*, 230c)—someone who, although he never ventured beyond the city limits, appears to behave like a foreigner (*xenagoumenoi*, 230c). Socrates loves learning from the men of the city, and seems to be reaffirming how philosophy as dialogue with others is essential to his life, rather than enquiry into the nature of the world. But this dialogue is not an "easy" conversation: it involves a position of foreignness—a speaker of a strange language, one nearly impossible to understand by most of his fellow citizens.

The philosopher and the *pharmakon*

The life and death of Socrates are marked by a very close relationship with *pharmakon*, translated as remedy, poison, drugs and medicine. Plato dedicated four dialogues to Socrates' death: the *Eutiphro*, in which he picks up the accusation against him and conducts a conversation with Eutiphro, expert in matters of piety; the *Apology,* where Socrates defends himself in front of his judges with a monologue on why he should not be condemned; the *Crito,* in which his friend Crito tries to convince him to escape from prison while he is awaiting trial; and the *Phaedo* in which Socrates celebrates his last philosophical conversation before his death. He wants to convince his friends that he is taking his soul to a new life, and that there is no reason for sadness. Death heralds a form of new life, a more free, pure and profound life. After talking to his friends, Socrates drinks the deadly *pharmakon.*

Other dialogues suggest a stronger association of Socrates' life with *pharmakon.* In a passage from the *Meno,* whose main topic of discussion is the nature of virtue (*arete*) and whether it can be taught, Meno accuses Socrates of having bewitched and drugged him (*geoteueis me kai pharmatteis,* 80a). Socrates accepts this. In the *Charmides,* a dialogue where Socrates talks about temperance (*sophrosyne*), with the young and beautiful Charmides, Critias presents Socrates as knowledgeable about the drug that can cure Charmides' headache ("caring for the soul with some potions", *epoidais tisin,* 157a). These testimonies exemplify the way in which different people viewed Socrates' proximity to *pharmakon.*

In the *Symposium,* which is an indirect narration of speeches celebrating love, Socrates (203ss.) portrays *Eros* as *daimon,* the intermediary being that passes life philosophizing, neither mortal (human being) nor immortal (God), a dreadful witch, wizard and sophist (*deinos goes kai pharmakeus kai sophistes,* 203d–e). Without doubt, it is a self-portrait: in many passages of the dialogues, Socrates displays these characteristics, including that of Agathon in the same *Symposium* (194a).

In the *Theaetetus,* Socrates meets the young Theatetus, who went on to be a prominent mathematician. There, Socrates says he has the same art as his mother, the midwife Fenareta, and he also mentions that midwives, using drugs (*pharmakia,* 149c) and potions, are able to provoke or alleviate the pain of childbirth, and deal with difficult births. Midwives have themselves given birth—they would not be able to help with something they themselves had never experienced. It is the same, says Socrates, in his art, with the difference that he makes men give birth to the examination of their souls, rather than their bodies. The most important of Socrates' art is his ability to be like the character Touchstone in Shakespeare's *As You Like It*—a wise fool putting everyone including himself to the comic test (*basanizein dynaton einai panti tropoi,* 150c).

The connection with midwifery is important to our theme because it suggests that, indirectly, through the analogy with his mother, Socrates is an expert in *pharmakia* and that *pharmakia* are essential for children (both literally and as a metaphor for knowledge) entering the world. Furthermore, it suggests that the use of *pharmakia* is essential to Socrates' practice. Although the way in which Plato describes this work in connection with knowledge of young people is similar to that of the *Phaedrus* (Socrates would consider whether youth gives birth to an image and a lie—simulacrum—or something fruitful and true, *eidolon kai pseudos…gonimon te kai alethes*, 150c), he can do so only because he is inspired by familiarity with the *pharmakon*, a familiarity that derives from his mother. This familiarity is a cornerstone of Socrates' ability.

As Derrida points out, there is no unity in the *pharmakon* (2000: 335). Rather, it is contradictory; its meaning is impossible to be fixed in one of its opposites without the presence of the other. In the case of a midwife, she can be the cause of life or death for a newborn, just as Socrates can produce life or death of new knowledge. The remedy is always a poison, a drug that can give life or cause death, depending on the dosage and circumstances. Plato, in the *Phaedrus*, confirms this contradictory nature, presenting the remedy (dialectic) as poison (writing, *graphe*). Socrates' proximity to the *pharmakon* means he too is affected by its contradictory nature. He seems unable to be fixed upon one identity without contradictions.

So Socrates' presentation at the beginning of the *Phaedrus* confirms his contradictory nature, as stated in other *dialogues*. Let's now read how he confronts the nature of writing in the sequence of the dialogue.

The condemnation of writing

Phaedrus reads Lysias' speech with great passion. Socrates argues against it in various ways. Regarding its form, he claims that it states the same things over and over, in different ways, like a child might (235a). Regarding its content, Socrates cites poets (Sappho and Anacreon) as possible sources of inspiration to speak better about the same subject. However, before criticizing Lysias' speech, he goes back to talking about himself, with his head covered to avoid embarrassment in front of Phaedrus: in order to understand Lysias' knowledge, Socrates argues, first the nature of love needs to be considered.

In the dialogue, an account follows of what Socrates himself later apologizes for, and adds another far more poetic, jubilant praise of Eros, this time with his face uncovered. This portrays philosophy as knowledge of and about love. Love is not only, or not mainly, an object of knowledge. Philosophy has passion within itself. Moreover, philosophy has within its name a word close to love—*philos*: passion, affection, friendship, also love, and *sophia*: knowledge.

Thereafter, Socrates criticizes Lysias and all authors of written speeches. Socrates clearly states that it is not embarrassing to write, but it is embarrassing to write poorly and without beauty (258d). It is therefore necessary to examine what it means to write well. Socrates discusses the relationship between rhetoric and truth, and analyses Lysias' speech in detail. He presents himself as a lover of the divisions and reconnections that allow him to speak and think. He is known as a "dialectician, capable of looking at one and many" (266b).

Socrates also proposes that Phaedrus consider whether it is appropriate to write (274b). He then tells a story of an Egyptian deity, Theuth, an inventor of numbers, arithmetic, geometry and astronomy, backgammon and dice, who presented the written characters (*grammata*, 274d) to King Thamus as a learning experience that would make Egyptians wiser and have greater memory.

He claims to have discovered what he described as a drug (*pharmakon*, 274e) for memory and wisdom.

However, the king questions the discovery. He claims that writing would have the opposite effect, causing forgetfulness in those who learn it, because by believing in external characters, they would neglect their own memory. According to Thamus, Theuth will have discovered a drug (*pharmakon*, 275a) for remembering (*hupomneseos*) and not for memory (*mneme*). The written word offers the appearance of knowledge, rather than true knowledge.

Here lies the basis of Platonism—the division of being into real being and derived being, model and simulation, original and copy, in epistemology, morality, politics. In all cases, the inferiority of the second compared with the first is categorical, basic and radical. The consequences are striking: it is necessary to know, protect and admire the first as much as to dislike, control and tackle the latter. I will now present Plato's argument against writing in its ontological dimension according to some contemporary criticism. Then I will link this discussion with two other issues that, according to Plato, are inseparable from writing—teaching and learning.

Like it or not, the philosopher writes. Indeed, Plato offers a loophole even when he signals the apparent negativity of writing. On the one hand, he points out several weaknesses, among which is the matter of dependency. Writing cannot defend itself independently (275e). It needs its writer. Furthermore, writing indiscriminately offers itself to its readers without being able to differentiate between those who are able to understand it and those who are not. Finally, writing may seem alive, but when questioned it cannot answer (275d), and always says the same thing. Curiously, the *pharmakon* is not pure imperfection. Plato writes that it is always one and the same, one of the most prominent kinds of ultimate truth, and in itself a mark of superiority and perfection because it does not change, unlike things that generate and corrupt themselves.

Furthermore, the issue of writing is familial and dialectic. Dialectic is called "the writing of the soul", the original model taking its name from the simulacrum (*eidolon*, 276a)! As Deleuze notes (1995: 295 ff.), moral judgment follows the duplication of legitimate and illegitimate. It is in this sense that Deleuze interprets the task of philosophy in the Nietzschean proposition of "inverted Platonism". This means denouncing the Platonic motivation to distinguish the world of essences from the world of appearances, and affirming the rights of the copies and the Simulacre to play the role of educators and governors in the *polis*. Plato establishes Unity and Semblance as models for judgment. Inverting Platonism means not making difference emerge from Unity, but having Unity emerge from difference (ibid.: 303). With this platonic gesture of naming the original after the copy, the battle appears lost before it even starts. This confirms the priority of difference in relation to a singular unit. The being is difference, despite Plato's will.

Plato would dream, says Derrida, with a memory without support, without sign, and without supplement (Derrida, 2000: 312), a memory that is a complete owner of its memories and of the activity of remembering.

In the Platonic perspective, writing—the support for memory—introduces a rift in being: one of a hybrid, a copy which cannot be thought according to the binary logic of being or not being, because, being a *pharmakon*, it is and is not at the same time. Writing introduces a crack in the intelligibility of what it is, an unnecessary, dangerous and seductive drug (*pharmakon*) which debilitates the strength and integrity of memory. The logos, as living being, suffers the external invasion of this parasite. It is necessary to remove it, and return it to its place. The dialectic is the platonic way of healing. The legitimate educator writes in the soul of the learner, is able to defend itself and knows when it is necessary to speak or to be silent. Compared with the dialectic, writing suffers from abandonment when the writer is absent.

Why does Plato so fiercely criticize writing in writing? Derrida has a hypothesis: writing should serve to cleanse itself; the *logos* should be cured of the writing parasite—through writing. This is Plato's boldness and his risk—philosophical, pedagogical and epistemological—because there is no science, episteme, of the *pharmakon*. Its essence is not to have a stable essence, but it is "the movement, the place and the game (the production) of the difference" (2000: 335). The *pharmakon* is an unfathomable reserve—a "bottomless pit"—the difference that "makes" all forms of differences, the differing of difference[4].

Thus, Plato drinks his own poison. According to Derrida the platonic opposites are derived from primordial writing—the *pharmakon* and the very first ("arqui-writing"). Writing is a "game of the other in being" (Derrida, 2000: 379). Plato writes because being cannot be one, because being is not a full and absolute presence. He writes because being can only be unfolding, repeating itself in what it is not, in simulacrum, subscribing itself to a repetitive structure to supplement an impossible unit. There is being—and truth—only because there is difference and repetition.

Writing and learning (through philosophy)

This condemnation of writing is not only a conceptual discussion but also a condemnation of certain tangible ways of practising writing. One of Plato's main problems is that certain rival intellectuals, educating youth in civic virtue, assume that learning and teaching virtue are both possible. They use writing to transmit forms of civic virtue which are quite different from what Plato wants for the *polis*.

For Plato the educator, writing as practiced by political rivals weakens the memory, the prime source of learning. In the *Meno*, he tells a story about how learning is remembering. The fundamental question is: is it indeed possible to teach *arete* (virtue; excellence)? Many say that it is and present themselves as capable of doing so. However, Plato makes Socrates call this claim into question. As usual, Socrates poses a condition before responding to the question: it is first necessary to know what *arête* is. Meno, an expert on speeches regarding *arete*, thinks he knows, but after just a few questions from Socrates he is stuck. He compares Socrates with a "stingray" that numbs its victims with electric shocks.

Socrates explains to Meno: "It is not because I myself am on the right track (*euporon*) that I leave others with no way out (*aporein*), but because I am myself more than anyone with no way out (*aporon*), that I also leave others with no way out (*aporein*)" (*Meno*, 80c–d). The contrast is between Socrates' two possible positions, respectively given by the prefix *eu* (well, good) and *a* (absence, need, negativity), similar to the same form *por,* which indicates movement, path, displacement. Socrates states that he problematizes others only because he is himself more problematized than anyone, and that this is because his knowledge is worthless just as the knowledge of others is worthless.

Is it possible to teach virtue or excellence? Socrates says that to teach virtue or excellence is to teach that one does not know what it is. There is no virtue or excellence to teach, unless it is the uneasy relationship with knowledge, a disturbance with what one knows, a manic search for knowledge while knowing nothing other than this not-knowing and the value of the search in itself. Only through self-questioning can an educator help others to question themselves. Only a virtuous person can lead others to virtue. Someone is virtuous who does not know the right path, is always seeking it, but never finding it, and even "knowing" that the right path is unknowable. Thus, from the Socratic perspective, it is possible to learn only by philosophizing. Only someone who is touched by philosophical questions, who questions why we live the life we live, can provoke this disquietude in others. This is why Socrates did not write anything; he had nothing to teach that could be fixed in writing. However, to question what one thinks can immobilize thinking. This is the paradox of learning shared by Socrates and his rivals. Learning seems impossible, for one can not learn what one already knows, and cannot learn what one does not know, for how would one recognize what one does not know?

Meno wants to know how to get out of this stalemate. Plato does not make Socrates help him—as a reader of the *Apology* would expect—by using his knowledge of not knowing, but feeds him with a theory taken from Pindar and other clerics, according to which the soul is immortal, and to investigate and learn are completely a matter of recall (*Meno*, 81d). How could Socrates know anything about the nature of soul? How could he know the essence of investigation and learning in such a different way from the position he maintains in other *dialogues*?

Meno asks Socrates to teach him about this theory. Plato has fun and makes Socrates respond: "Now, you ask me if I can teach you, when I told you that teaching is nothing but remembering" (82a). Socrates asks Meno to bring a servant (a slave that was not purchased, but raised in the house from birth) who speaks Greek to show how in fact he teaches nothing. During the course of the conversation, the slave becomes convinced of the perplexity of a false knowledge he previously had, and this perplexity inspires in him the desire to learn more about what he now recognized as a problem. As a result, he learns new (mathematical) content, a different knowledge that, according to Socrates, he already knew but did not remember. Socrates concludes with a question that could be answered only in an affirmative way: "Without anyone having taught him, and only through questions put to him, he will understand, recovering the knowledge out of himself?" (*Meno*, 85d).

We could question various things: whether or not the conclusion is a legitimate one? Whether indeed no one taught the servant what he learns, and whether he learns that which he knows or that which Socrates knows? We could also ask what other things he learns from Socrates, besides mathematical knowledge. However, what interests me here is that Plato has Socrates resolve the stalemate on the side of knowing, using learning as an aid to memory. One can teach only knowledge that the other already knows, helping to remind him of what he already knows but has forgotten. This is the Platonic solution to the paradox: to learn is to reconnect with knowledge that one already has. Thus, for Plato, in the deteriorating state of the *polis*, learning becomes not just possible, but necessary, and essential to finding forgotten knowledge that helps to turn what is into what ought to be.

In the exercise with Meno, it is interesting that while Socrates does not write, he does need to draw a figure in the ground, to help Meno remember his knowledge. In any case, if it is indeed true that writing debilitates memory, then writing puts learning at risk. Without learning there is no possibility of finding out what ought to be, and hence no chance of transforming the way in which we live. If memory is essential to learn (remember) the perfect realm of forms, then writing threatens the platonic aspirations of a more fair, beautiful and true *polis* through the education of childhood.

In the *Pheadrus* this takes on new dimensions. The criticism of writing assumes a pedagogical and political battlefield in the formation of Athenian childhood. Interestingly, Plato's adversaries are not only the writers of speeches but also his teacher who, as we have seen, takes a position that contains not only difference but also tension, paradox and contradiction. Thus, Plato fights not only those who claim to know what virtue is and how to teach it, but also his own teacher Socrates who claims one cannot know what virtue is and cannot teach it.

Derrida suggests something interesting: it is true that Plato condemning writing would condemn those who accuse Socrates through writing. However, it would also condemn Socrates' actual position (2000: 366), a way of practicing a philosophical life compared with a sterile and passive political life. Then, the condemnation of writing would have the double effect of condemning Socrates' accusers, but also Socrates' position itself as one of a philosopher educator of childhood, as someone who educates, in the name of philosophy, without teaching—a kind of learning that does not lead to the kind of knowing that Plato considers essential to the sort of political transformation that education of the young should bring to the *polis*.

This dichotomy comprises two philosophies: philosophy as a way of learning to question knowledge; and philosophy as a means to acquire positive knowledge crucial for living a good life. Philosophy as questioning politics is placed before philosophy as a claim of normative knowledge for the *polis*. The foreign and atopic philosopher would be impotent, in the platonic vision, to find the political means to transform the state of affairs. Plato seems unwilling to accept Socrates' position, and this is his reason for writing the *dialogues* and founding the Academy.

It is not an issue of taking sides. However, the battle seems lost for Plato before it has begun. Philosophy, like *pharmakon*, resists capture. There is a closet Socrates in every platonic teacher, who smiles at the formative pretensions of the philosophical, pedagogical institutionalization of childhood, and welcomes the *pharmakon,* questioning and *philos*. The Socratic educator does not teach, but provokes learning. She understands the value of not knowing, of always desiring to know differently, in a life that is worth living. Such an educator does not form childhood, but acts as a childlike educator and makes education childlike. She creates the conditions under which childhood can educate. She enables the difference of childhood to be learned and written in educational practice.

Pharmakon, childhood and philosophy

Pharmakon as a contradiction, as the anti-substance, is a challenge to Plato's logic of thinking. It is something that such logic cannot deal with. Childhood plays a similar role in the *dialogues,* as I will justify in the following paragraphs. In several of them, the question of childhood education appears in a significant way, for example in the *Laches, Protagoras, Alcibiades I, Gorgias, Meno* and, particularly, in the *Republic.* Plato is always motivated by the same concern— that Athenians suffer the political consequences of a bad education; the *polis* is unfair because it has not had the knowledge to educate its childhood and, consequently, has not provided its childhood with the knowledge necessary to transform it. The implication is that the sole means to save the *polis* is to educate children with true knowledge.

Education exists only because there is childhood, and because we are not born educated and ready for public life. For Plato, this statement could be translated as follows: education exists because we are not born as fair, good and beautiful as we could be. In the *dialogues,* the state of childhood is seen in the realms of ethics, aesthetics, epistemology and politics as a flaw, a problem, a sign of inferiority. For example, in the *Alcibiades I* 110a–c, Socrates criticizes Alcibiades for presuming to know what is righteous and unrighteous "even as a child", taking for granted that as long as he is a child he cannot be part of the world of the fair and unfair. He speaks glowingly of Charmides, and confirms his exceptional character, that at his young age he does not have the negative qualities of a child (*Charmides* 154b). He is an exceptional child mainly because he is almost not a child. In the *Gorgias*, Socrates accuses Callicles of treating him like a child, by opposing him through contradictory statements (499b–c), and by claiming that the speakers, who seek to please citizens without regard to public interest, treat them like children (502e). The same adverb *paidia* is used in various *dialogues* as a synonym for childish, naïve and weak (*Crito* 46d; *Gorgias* 470c, 471d; *Symposium* 204b).

In the *Gorgias*, the devaluing of childhood is associated with a criticism of philosophy. Callicles asks Socrates to stop acting like a child and to distance himself from philosophy in order to dedicate himself to more important matters (*Gorgias* 484c). He says that philosophy corrupts men when they remain in it too long, and that it makes them inexperienced (*apeiron*) for public life in the *polis*. He claims that those who philosophize too much do not know the laws, do not know how to treat other people, and are not transparent, not well regarded and experienced (*empeiron*). In sum, they are ridiculous in public and private affairs (*Gorgias* 484c–d) in which they behave like children. This is what happens to Socrates who behaves like a child in the *polis*. The philosopher is as ridiculous and childlike in public affairs as politicians are in philosophical conversations. Callicles offers a comparison:

> It is a fine thing to partake of philosophy just for the sake of education, and it is no disgrace for a lad to follow it: but when a man already advancing in years continues in its pursuit, the affair, Socrates, becomes ridiculous; and for my part I have much the same feeling towards students of philosophy as towards those who lisp or play tricks. For when I see a little child, to whom it is still natural to talk in that way, lisping or playing some trick, I enjoy it, and it strikes me as pretty and ingenuous and suitable to the infant's age; whereas if I hear a small child talk distinctly, I find it a disagreeable thing, and it offends my ears and seems to me more befitting a slave.
>
> (485a–b, translated by B. Jowett)

Callicles states that it is beautiful to dedicate oneself to philosophy to the extent that it serves education (*paideia*). Not that there is any appreciation for the two: they can be together only because they are both, by nature, unimportant, or, at best, a preparation for what really matters: the political life of adults. In Callicles' view, education refers to a world prior to the entry into politics. There is no politics in education; therefore philosophy can accompany it during childhood because it too is outside the world of politics.

In the *Republic*, Adeimantus offers a similar argument: those who do not abandon philosophy after embracing it as part of their education when they are children (*neoi*), become adults who are strange (*allokotuous*) or evil people (the *Republic* VI 487c–d). Philosophy can be practiced while one is young, but politics is the world of the mature, which is where philosophy is out of place. When in the *Republic*, philosophy is included at an older age in the curriculum of politicians aspiring to govern the *polis*, it is philosophy as theoretical knowledge, very different from the practical philosophy practised by Socrates.

The philosopher, childlike, is also a stranger. We have seen how the *Phaedrus* presents it in this way. Derrida states that to show oneself as a stranger is Socrates' game (1997: 19), and illustrates this by recalling a passage from the *Apology,* at the beginning of Socrates' defence. In court, Socrates declares himself a completely foreigner to the lexicon of the place (*atechnos oun xenos echo tes enthade lexeos*, 17e). As such, he tells the judges that he will speak using the same words as he is used to doing in the present moment, together with the vendors in the marketplace (*dia ton auton logon*, 17c). He therefore requests to be allowed to speak in the voice (*phone*) with which he was raised, as if he truly were a foreigner. Socrates would speak in a philosopher's voice—the voice of childhood. The democratic Athenian judges would not listen to a foreigner, a child and a philosopher. There is no common language between Socrates and the judges. Socrates speaks the true word of childhood; his judges, the false word of rhetoric. The *polis* is insensitive to the childlike language of the philosopher. It cannot hear the childhood educating voice.

Let's summarize the path of this chapter. I first presented the way in which Plato describes the philosopher and the conditions for philosophical dialogue in the *Phaedrus*. I then showed how the philosopher is close to the nature of the *pharmakon* in some *dialogues* of Plato. After presenting Plato's critique of writing in the *Phaedrus,* I put it in the context of Plato's battle on the education of childhood. We realized there how crucial the issue is for Plato: writing threatens memory and through it, learning and the educational project that will lead to political utopia. In this regard, Plato even confronted his beloved master Socrates because his position in relation to knowledge was not strong enough to warrant having philosophers rule the *polis*. Socrates was too child-like and too open to the lack of certainty in his philosophical life. Finally, I've just pointed out the similar position played by childhood and philosophy in relation to the political realm as presented in the *dialogues*.

Then, unless we want to retake a Platonic path, would do neither philosophy nor childhood any favors by placing them in the realm of childhood citizenship education. That path promises the conversion of childhood into adulthood and of philosophy from a questioning life into theoretical knowledge. If philosophy and childhood are on the same side in the battle in the *dialogues*, it is because they both affirm the dangerous ontological and political force of difference. In this sense, the political force of Socrates' philosophy lies in its childhood form: it does not know, but always desires to know; it does not teach but generates others' learning and does not give form but enables a self-forming pathway.

In its Socratic, childlike and foreign ways of expressing itself in a community, philosophy shows the value of searching for knowledge above all other things, of questioning and unlearning what we know and affirming the value of not knowing, of attempting to respond, with all of its forces, to those questions which cannot be answered. This practice of philosophy is not knowledge but a relationship to knowledge.

Understood in this way, philosophy is useless for constructing a political-pedagogical project. In Plato's view, it is not only useless: it is also dangerous. Because of this, it must be purged from the *polis,* because it leaves no good place for a curriculum, for a development of learning, which can make the *polis* more beautiful, good and fair, as Plato claims it ought to be. However, every condemnation reaffirms the value of the condemned. Childhood and philosophy persist like a *pharmakon*. Several worlds open up: in philosophy, in education and in politics.

This form of philosophy is not free from some tensions: how can we know that what we know is not true or good knowledge? Is there any knowledge valuable other than the knowledge of not knowing? From where does the value of childhood, philosophy and difference arise? Are there good and bad differences, good and bad relationships to knowledge? If so, from what point could we make these kinds of judgments? Can we in any way assess a philosophical dialogue, question or life? If so, from which standpoint? Has philosophy any role in evaluating different ways of life? If so, how?

These questions are not easy to answer. I'll not try to answer them not only because they call for other readings, but mainly because ending this chapter with questions is also a way of affirming the priority of childhood, difference and philosophy as understood by Socrates. Moreover, these questions could themselves be questioned: what are their presuppositions? Don't they presuppose a Platonic image of thinking[5], which is exactly what needs to be questioned? How would these questions be questioned in a way more sensitive to childhood and difference? What new questions would emerge? What new forms of thinking are needed to make them possible?

If childhood, philosophy and difference have shown their force in this exercise of writing and reading, I rely on the reader not to expect me not just to answer but even not to pose any of these questions.

Notes

1 Poison, drug, medicine, remedy (Liddell and Scott, 1966).
2 City, State, City-State.
3 Inspired by Derrida and Deleuze, here I understand difference in itself, i.e., difference not in relation to anything else "different from..." but as such, difference as difference. For Derrida's way of raising the problem, see infra n. 7.
4 Derrida affirms that *pharmakon* is a reservation of difference, what "produces" difference in oppositions and in any other difference, something like what makes "difference" differ from "the *différance of difference*". On the concept of *différance*, cf Derrida (1968). « La différance », published in the *Bulletin de la société française de philosophie* (juillet-septembre 1968) and in *Théorie d'ensemble* (coll. Tel Quel), Ed. du Seuil,
5 The expression comes from Deleuze's critique of Western Philosophy, in Chapter 3 of *Difference and Repetition* (Deleuze, 1968).

Bibliography

Deleuze, G. (1968) *Différence et Répétition*. Paris: PUF.
———. (1995) 'Platon te le simulacre' in *Logique du sens*. Paris: Les Éditions de Minuit.
Derrida, J. (1980) *La carte postale*. Paris: Flammarion.
———. (1997) *De l'hospitalité*. Anne Dufourmantelle invite Jacques Derrida à répondre. Paris: Calmann-Lévy.
———. (2000) 'La pharmacie de Platon' in Platon, *Phèdre*. Trans. L. Brisson. Paris: GF-Flammarion, pp 255–403.
Liddell, H. and Scott, R. (1966) *A Greek English Lexicon*. Oxford: Clarendon Press.
Plato (1989) *The Dialogues of Plato*. Trans. B. Jowett. New York: Oxford University Press.

Afterword

The pedagogue and/or the philosopher?
An exercise in thinking together: a dialogue
with Jan Masschelein

This conversation took place via email during the last months of 2013 and the early days of 2014. Given our very busy agendas it was planned as a non-pretentious and undemanding exercise. In fact it was just that, but something about it so attracted our attention and interest that it also it turned out to be an intense and touching encounter, through which not just the conversation but our relationship grew. Maybe because we were raising topics that turned out to be something approaching existential obsessions for both of us, or maybe for some other reason, we became deeply involved in what might be called (not without hesitation) a truly philosophical and/or educational dialogue.

WALTER OMAR KOHAN: After reading your characterization of educational research as having three main dimensions: a) concerning something educational; b) making something public; and c) leading to the transformation of the researcher, I found myself asking how this would be different from philosophical research. In your preface to the Brazilian Edition of *Pedagogy, Democracy, School* (Masschelein, J., 2014, in press), you respond to that question, affirming that true philosophical research is in fact educational research, and the other way around. I find this a fascinating topic. On the one hand, I also see philosophy as education and cannot separate the two, but on the other, I am not all that convinced that we shouldn't establish some kind of distinction between them—a distinction I am not completely clear about. But I would say that if the questions "what is philosophy?" and "what is education?" have different answers—and I think they have—then there should be a distinction between those two concepts. The issue can be also raised by focusing on the figure of the professor of philosophy, who in a sense is located between philosophy and education, and practices philosophy as education. I remember Foucault's last course on *parrhesia*, *Le courage de la vérité* (Foucault, 2009), where he gives some lectures on Socrates, and in one of the last moments of those lectures, he indirectly characterizes himself as a professor of philosophy. His tone is very supportive of Socrates and suggests a kind of identification: both are parrhesiasts, close to death, speaking a truth their societies do not want to hear. There, Foucault inscribes himself in the tradition inaugurated by Socrates in which philosophy is not knowledge but a problematization of life, a way of living, a form of "giving reasons" (*didonai logoi*) for one's own way of life. According to Foucault (2009), Socrates as a professor of philosophy occupies a singular and paradoxical position: he takes care of himself by not taking care *ipso facto* of himself, but by taking care that all the others take care of themselves. So, in a sense, he does not care for himself literally but, in another sense, he is the one who takes more care than anyone else in the *polis* because he takes care of the care of everybody. This is, according to Foucault, what makes a philosopher an educator or Socrates a teacher of philosophy. In this sense, Socrates would be very far from the Platonic image of the teacher of philosophy as someone who confirms that the other is in need of the philosopher "to get out of the cave". I would rather say that "the inaugural gesture of philosophy" in a Socratic sense is rather "you need to care of what you do not care for" and this is what gives meaning and sense to a philosophical life, which needs to be at the same time an educational life. If Socrates educated the others it is because, after talking to Socrates, they realized they could no longer live the life they were living. In this sense, I think Rancière's critique of Socrates in *The Ignorant Schoolmaster* (Rancière, 1987) is interesting but at the same time partial and problematic. It is true if we take Plato's *Meno* as Rancière does, but in many other *dialogues* Socrates' position is much more complex and less arrogant and hierarchical, and Socrates acts as if the other is equally capable of engaging in a form of dialogue that promises to lead out of the cave. Here Socrates is saying something like: be attentive, you also can live another life, you also can take care. I wonder how you consider this way of thinking the relationship between philosophy and education. What do you think?

JAN MASSCHELEIN: Walter, allow me to start with recalling some points of what I wrote to you earlier. Just as a start. As I told you then, I forgot that Foucault called himself a professor of philosophy in that course. You know I listened to the recordings of these lectures for days and days in the beginning of 2000 and it was really a strong moment for me, since indeed in some of these (and especially in *The Hermeneutics of the Self* (Foucault, 2001), which I think is one of the great books of "philosophy as education" together indeed with the lectures on *parrhesia*) he shows us the possibility of a different and intriguing reading of Socrates (and some others) which, although he was inspired by Pierre Hadot (1993), was in various ways more interesting and challenging than Hadot's (including the way in which Foucault interpreted Socrates' last words, commenting on Dumézil's interpretation). And I agree with you that this understanding of Socrates is, so to say, different, even strongly different from the Platonic one. And just like you, in the courses in which I discuss Rancière I try to show how I think he is commenting only on a certain Socrates (amazing to see once more how close I come to your thinking), who of course is present in many of the *dialogues*, but that there is also another

Socrates, who one could indeed say is starting from equality—to use his phrase—and who, as you say, is much more complex. However, Foucault also tries to explain in his lectures (Foucault, 2009) how this Socrates is probably closer to the cynics, and how this line of "philosophy" (if we can call it this) has remained marginal and maybe ended up finally more in the arts (and maybe in some mystics) than in what is more commonly called "philosophy". It is also the case that in the time of Socrates all these notions of "philosophy", "sophism", "poetry", etc. were still very much unclear and struggled over. And maybe I am giving too much weight to the Platonic "beginning" of philosophy, not as a "doctrine" or a "theory" or "conviction", but as a fundamental *gesture* (which in my thinking is always a remnant of some aristocracy), which finds its place in academia. In fact I have difficulties not recognizing this gesture in most philosophers. Of course, I like philosophy and also want to remain related to philosophy (and Foucault offered in a sense the direction in which such a relation might be established and maintained), but on the other hand, I think that it also often hinders us and makes us blind to the figure of the pedagogue and even leads us to despise that figure, whereas I believe more and more that the pedagogue (as the one that takes one out of the home to the school—he is in that sense an educator—and attends the school to make sure that it remains a school) is more important for democracy and for "humanity" (which are, I know, enormous words) than the "philosopher" so called, and that this figure of the pedagogue (which, I admit, is maybe also to be seen as a philosopher in a totally different way, but again: to go too quickly to "philosophy" make us forget other things too easily) offers a better starting point for developing a "philosophy of/ as education" which goes beyond the recurrent move to derive so-called educational consequences out of philosophical thought. The more I think about it—and I must confess that this thinking has profited from my conversations with Maarten—the more I believe that in a certain way philosophy has been a way not only of taming democracy (which is in fact the source of Rancière's hatred of democracy, but could also be related to Foucault's reading of what happened to the Socratic *parrhesia* after his death), but also of taming the school, or to say it in a less provocative or aggressive way, to forgetting the school, and to neglecting its crucial public character (or to say it in a different way, with Maarten: school is the unthought of philosophy). Hopefully, we can understand this more clearly in our further conversation, although we will certainly need different sallies and approaches, and will end up now and then at dead ends. And I want also to keep in mind the studies which deal not with Socrates but with Isocrates, which try to show that in fact there was a argument going on about who could actually claim to be a philosopher, and what it meant—an argument which Isocrates lost, so to say, in the long run, in that he was more and more understood as a teacher/educator. So, let me take up what you wrote—that is, Socrates as the one who says: "you need to take care of what you do not care for" and Socrates as an educator in that, after talking to him, people realized they could no longer live the life they were living. These phrases recall for me a wonderful book which you might know of, recently published by Peter Sloterdijk, called *You Must Change Your Life* (2013) (in German: *Du muss Dein Leben ändern*). He borrows these words from a famous poem by Rilke (1908), which he wrote after having seen an armless torso in a museum in Paris. What is interesting is that Rilke precisely seems to indicate that here there is a command coming out of the stone—an appeal that says that you can no longer live the life you are living, that you must change it. This command is not one that limits or prohibits, but nevertheless it sends a message that cannot be denied. As such it issues from a kind of authority that has nothing to do with a social position, role or function, but is both aesthetic and ethical (not moral) in one: Rilke says that the torso is perfect—"*volkommen*"—and Sloterdijk suggests that it works as a model, not to imitate, but nevertheless as an impetus. And although I think that of course you can speak of some educational experience here that produces a need to change and take care (of what you do not care for), this is for me in a way already too ethical a reading, or to say it differently: an ethical reading threatens to hide or conceal the educational reading and experience, which does not have the structure of an immediate command (you *must* change your life), but refers to the dis-closure of world and the dis-covery of an (im-)potentiality (you *are* not un-able). For me these two aspects (dis-closure of world, i.e. making public, and dis-covery of (im)-potentiality) are essential to an educational experience, and I am no longer sure whether or not the Socratic conversation contains these two elements. I don't know whether this is understandable to any extent. Let us say that this is just a very first commentary on the idea that philosophy and education are different, a claim with which in fact I agree. My point is rather that a philosophical reading of education tends to discard an educational or pedagogical reading, and tends to take different experiences as its starting point. Maybe this is something we could develop further, related to the experience of wonder or stupefaction which many associate with philosophy (and study), whereas I think that there is an experience of being attracted and of being not unable which is associated with education. But, as I said, maybe I am already confused? What do you think?

WOK: Thanks for your answer, Jan, which is not at all confusing, quite the contrary, it's very inspiring. You touch on a very interesting point about philosophy that has to do with it as a "fussy" kind or dimension of thinking, something that makes us feel we do not want to be out of it but at the same time does not allow us to feel really comfortable inside it; as if philosophy contains—at least in its dominant form—its own negation, that is, the non philosophical. And it is indeed ironic that this discourse speaks in the name of "real" philosophy, and condemns and excommunicates whatever does not speak its language—as if some power were speaking in the name of philosophy in a voice that inhibits philosophy itself, at least that form of philosophy initiated by Socrates and affirmed, among others, by the cynics. This is probably why, as you said, it might be easier to find the philosophical in art than in philosophy itself, which is another dimension of its enigmatic nature. So even if it is true that in the name of philosophy, democracy, schooling, so many other important things have been tamed, forgotten and neglected, we can still question whether we need to accept this domestication as truly philosophical. But let's focus on your line of thinking when you question whether we could find in Socratic conversation the two aspects you propose—"dis-closure of world, i.e. making public, and dis-covery of (im-)potentiality"—as both important and "essential" for an educational experience. I am tempted to answer your question positively but I would rather propose that we consider together a passage from the *Lysis* where, it seems to me, your line of argument is addressed. Socrates has been speaking first with Hippothales, pointing out how inconvenient his tactic of flattering his beloved Lysis is. When Socrates talks to Lysis himself (Plato, *Lysis* 207b ff.) he puts his own tactic into practice, opposite to the one of Hippothales, of *un*flattering Lysis by showing him that a real *phílos* loves someone not because of his physical beauty but because he thinks accurately (*phronein*, 210d). And, interestingly enough, the way he proves to Lysis that he does not think accurately is by pointing out that he has a teacher (*didaskalou*, 210d). First he asks Lysis if his parents allow him to "conduct/govern himself" (*archein seautou*, 208c), to which Lysis answers negatively, saying that a pedagogue (*paidagogos*), a slave, does it, as you say, conducting him to the teacher. Now, it seems to me that both of your conditions are present in this conversation with Lysis. In his claim that thinking accurately and not physical beauty is what makes someone free, Socrates discloses a dimension of the world that Lysis has not paid attention to before, and in so doing, discovers an (im-)potentiality in Lysis, which he turns into such a potentiality that after talking to Socrates, Lysis vows that he is going to talk about what he previously ignored with Menexenus. This passage shows a clear defence by Socrates of the role of the teacher, which seems to be related to the need of the student to think accurately. This passage makes me think than when Socrates says he has never been a teacher of anyone—as in Plato's *Apology* 33a—he is not doing a critique of education from the outside—in the name of philosophy—but rather of a certain way of being a teacher, characteristic of those teaching in Athens at the time. In contradistinction to these, Socrates receives no money for dialoguing with others, he claims to teach no knowledge, and no one can say that they learned something different in private from him than they learned in public, as we read in the *Apology* 33a–c. In this passage of the *Apology* Socrates says that 1) he does not teach, and that 2) others learn with him, which implies at least two things: a) he is involved in an educational task; b) he does something different from "normal" teachers, not teaching knowledge but teaching others to pay attention to a dimension of the world they do not see, as he does with Lysis, thereby empowering or potentiating others. At the same time, Socrates seems to be doing with Lysis what Rilke identifies with emerging from the stone—an appeal to change the way someone is living. Like Rilke's stone, Socrates does not speak from any particular social position or role but as an aesthetic voice, which also seems to carry an ethical commandment. I am not sure I would say "you must change your life", but at least "if you do not change your life, your life loses something valuable to the world and you lose your own potency/ potential", to put it in your educational words. So, in a sense I would say it is both a pedagogical (educational) and an ethical/aesthetic presence in Socrates, which makes me wonder whether we really can separate the two. There is also an interesting passage in Plato's *Laches* where Nicias argues to Lysimachus that whoever encounters Socrates needs to give an account of the kind of life he lives and to be more careful for the rest of his life, and adds that it is quite familiar and pleasant for him "to rub upon the touchstone" (*basanizesthai, Laches* 188b) of Socrates. Again, here Socrates seems to be promoting a kind of energy directed toward changing and taking care of one's life, as you put it, and we see that both the educational and the aesthetic/ethical seemed to be addressed. I wonder how you read these passages, Jan. I haven't read Isocrates and would love it if you could dis-cover this im-potentiality in me by offering some texts that relate to how he conceived of this narrative. But I see Socrates—at least one of the many Socrates whom we can read in the *dialogues*—as an educator through his philosophical life, meaning someone who provokes in the other the impossibility of continuing to live as he was living before, in terms of a disclosure of the world and a potentiality in oneself. If I've given so much attention to Socrates here, it is not for the character himself, but what he allows us to think (or might I say how he still educates us in?) this relationship between philosophy and education. He seems to be affirming what you consider to be a philosophical and educational experience and, at the same time he is suggesting that we cannot leave any of them out if we mean to live a truly educational life. Is Socrates too much of a mythical, exceptional, unique figure? Or might he lead us to reconsider how we define the educational and the philosophical? I would like to read what you think about this. And concerning the *pathos* connected with this educational/philosophical experience, I suggest that you consider two words: *questioning* and *dissatisfaction*, both of which, it seems to me, are critical to understanding Socrates as philosopher and as educator. Am I too confusing now, Jan?

JM: Dear Walter, thank you very much for your wonderful reading and remarks. And certainly also for making me read this passage in the *Lysis*—I should say reread, since apparently I must have read it at some point (I find my notes in the text and I have even particularly marked the section you refer to), but I must confess that I totally forgot, so that I couldn't even recall it when I read your response the first time. But, it is indeed a really interesting passage, which offers many possibilities for reconsidering the position (and valuation) of the "slave" and the pedagogue/teacher, and I can agree almost in all senses with the way you suggest reading it. Let me, for now, try to take up two or three points in your response.

The first is regarding "love". Your use of *"philos"* (the real *philos*) made me consider whether we could add another element to our discussion regarding this form of love. You state that the real *"philos"* "loves someone not because of his physical beauty but because he thinks accurately (*phronein*)". Immediately many things come to mind, and although they could carry us away us away from our issue, let me say a few things nevertheless. It is interesting that the combination you suggest here is not *"philosophia"* but *"philophronein"*. Of course the issue of *"philia"* is important in itself (in these times especially it seems more than worthwhile to recall that education/philosophy has to do with a certain kind of love), but I think it is also important to consider the "object" (or "subject"—it is difficult to find the right word, since it also relates to the direction of the force that is at work here). This could be elaborated in different ways, but for the purposes of our dialogue it might be worthwhile not only to go into this distinction between *sophia* and *phronein* (nor would it be difficult to show how Isocrates is always questioning "Sophia" in relation to human affairs and proclaiming *"phronein"*—to which he relates his "school"), but also to consider the possibility of a *"philo-kosmos"*. Let me try to be a bit more precise. As you know, Foucault explicitly refers to the *Alcibiades I* in order to argue that Socrates has a particular kind of love for his "student" (forgive me if I insert a thought that comes up now: maybe one cannot use this word in this context, it might be better to use "pupil" or .....?), explaining that Socrates is addressing Alcibiades not out of love for his beauty, for his body, for his wealth, etc., but out of love for "himself" (for, so to say, his soul)—and this is also what resonates in the passage of the *Lysis* to some extent. But now that you specify that he loves someone for thinking accurately, I would be interested in how you relate these two (I mean love for himself as such and love for thinking accurately—and one can probably understand this as someone who is taking care of himself): is the love conditional? Furthermore, there is the issue of the world. As you know, Hannah Arendt, who didn't want to be called a philosopher, criticised almost the entire philosophical tradition (including thinkers such as Seneca, to whom Foucault refers in his late works) for its "hatred" of the world—she herself always proclaiming an "amor mundi" (*"philo-kosmos"* if that translation could be made). In her famous text on the crisis in education (Arendt, 1958), she describes education as related to this double love for the world and for the younger generation (which I think is not the love for "my" son or daughter, but rather any "son" or "daughter"). I must say that I am still unsure whether or at least to what extent the *"philos"* that Socrates is, is a *"philos"* of the world; and whether the *philos* is not first of all a *philos* of himself (implying that perhaps *philos* of *sophia*—but maybe not of *phronein*?—is finally also a form of self-love). You will recall that Rancière (1987) accuses the Socrates of the *Apology* of arrogance—at least towards the end: that he starts with the assumption of inequality, and that he prefers to save his own virtue, which you could interpret to mean that he loves himself (his own soul and *"sophia"*) more than the world, and is disdainful or contemptuous of the others (*"le mépris"*) (and it is interesting to note that Isocrates, in his fictional apologia, the *Antidote*, in defending himself before an imaginary court, is addressing the audience in a totally different way). Or, more directly related to the issue of "world-disclosure", I am not really convinced that this contempt is an issue in the passage of the *Lysis*. Of course, we can discuss what it means, but I have the impression that what you call "a dimension of the world" that Lysis had not paid attention to before is not so much a dimension of the world (some "thing"—in the Heideggerian sense of "thing"—outside himself), but rather a dimension of himself. I am aware that Foucault was always was consciously trying to connect care of the self to care of the world, but I must say that I continue to have difficulty seeing that at work in Socrates, although he often explicitly confirms his role (but is that also out of love?) in the *polis*. Of course he states in the *Apology* that he is taking care of the city, that he is a "blessing" for the city, but is that the same? I simply don't know or am not sure.

Nevertheless, I agree with you that this figure of the "touchstone" is very strong and remains fascinating, and yes, as you say, maybe there he is an educator (and yes, he seems also to reveal something, which has more to do with *"phronein"* than with *"sophia"*); but then the question comes up again, what *is* the difference between the educator and the philosopher, and are we maybe discussing two ways of conceiving of philosophy as education? Maybe we should explore a bit what you call "the philosophical" life, which, since it would offer a touchstone, would in itself be educational. I think this is certainly a very interesting idea (although I am still uncertain to what extent and in what sense it addresses the issue of "the world"), and it can be related to the kind of authority that Rilke was talking about. And maybe we should also think what the philosophical life has to do with school?

Let me leave it there for now, after just one note regarding Isocrates: I am not a specialist myself, and many things are unclear, disputable, contradictory, etc. (as is of course the case with many interesting texts and figures), but the little text *"Against the Sophists"* and his *"The Antidosis"* seem to me to be good ways to get into his thinking, which is concerned to revaluate sophism and public speech—albeit, surprisingly, precisely by claiming the importance of writing.

WOK: Dear Jan, thank you for making me read Isocrates, which is really interesting and surprising! I followed your advice and read *"Against the*

Sophists" and "*The Antidosis*". His writing is very thoughtful and provocative. I particularly enjoyed the latter which has clear parallels with
Plato's *Apology,* Socrates and Isocrates both identifying their prosecution
as a prosecution of philosophy (*The Antidosis* 170), defending themselves
in old age in the name of truth against "unfair" accusations (real, in the
case of Socrates, fictional for Isocrates). Interestingly, like Socrates,
Isocrates makes it explicit in the last part of the introduction that his
speech will show the truth about himself. Even the accusations against
him are very similar to those made against Socrates, not only in their
content but also in the spirit of their rejoinders. Even the arrogant tone is
similar (for example: "Now for this I deserved praise rather than preju-
dice", ibid.: 152). Isocrates is also very close to Socrates in one important
way regarding our conversation: he puts himself in a superior position to
all human beings, not because of *sophia* but because he considers himself
the "cleverest" or "most expert" (*deinotatos*) and because he is a writer of
speeches (*sunngraphes ton logon*). He even identifies himself as naturally
superior in speech-making and praxis (for Isocrates, it seems, nature comes
before all else, ibid.: 189), and his feeling of superiority seems even
stronger than Socrates'. In section 162 he gives reasons for this: "I thought
that if I could acquire a greater competence and attain a higher position
than others who had started in the same profession, I should be acclaimed
both for the superiority of my teaching and for the excellence of my conduct." Note that the word for "profession" is *bios* and for "teaching",
philosophia. So I do not want to pressure you to go back to Isocrates now,
but I would very much like it if one day you could make it more explicit
in what sense Isocrates addresses the audience "in a totally different way"
than Socrates. This is not to neglect the differences: as you pointed out,
Isocrates is writing his defence, whereas Socrates wrote nothing at all.
Isocrates acknowledges having had many disciples (*mathetas,* ibid., 87, 98)
and unlike Socrates he describes himself as someone who teaches (*didasko,*
ibid., 89). He establishes some conditions for accepting students: natural
aptitude, prior formation and knowledge of the sciences (*episteme*), and
their practice (*empeiria,* 187). His understanding of philosophy is complex,
but very different from Socrates', associated as it is with oratory. He seems
to have a very specific and particular notion of philosophy. I am aware
that I've performed a very superficial reading and could be talking non-
sense but to be sincere, it seems to me that Socrates is much closer to your
conception of philosophy as education than Isocrates is. Even "love"
doesn't seem to play such a special role in Isocrates as it does in Socrates.
Concerning your question about love, Foucault and the *Alcibiades,* I read
Foucault as stressing that Socrates' love is not for Alcibiades himself but of
Alcibiades' way of being in the world (if we can say that) as guided by
care. In other words, the "object" (as you said, the word here is difficult)
of Socrates' love is not Alcibiades himself but Alcibiades taking care of or
being occupied with himself: with Alcibiades living a certain kind of life

or existence (see, for example, Foucault, 2001: 38). In the *Alcibiades I* Plato marked this love as a love of someone's soul, being the soul what most properly characterizes a human being (129e–130a). But as Foucault has also pointed out in some other *dialogues* such as the *Laches,* it is clear that Socrates was more in love with a way of life. As Alcibiades is not living this kind of life, Socrates' love has this pedagogical dimension in which the lover takes care of the beloved, cares for his caring, relates to him in a way that encourages him to take care of what he does not really care about. This is what Foucault calls the "pedagogical deficit" under which Socrates inscribes his task—in other words, this is philosophy as pedagogy, loving as the generative force of a kind of existence or life. Again, I am aware that Foucault distinguished two possibilities present in Plato's *dialogues* concerning the care of the self. In one case—*Alcibiades I*—the care of the self is understood as knowledge of the self and, more precisely, of the most important part of the self, which for Plato is the soul. In another case—the *Laches,* to which we already referred—the care of the self is understood as being able to give an account of a certain way of life. Foucault opposes these two possibilities because according to him they give birth to two different ways of understanding and practicing philosophy: one as cognitive or intellectual activity and another as the aesthetics of existence or *askesis,* as you referred to it before. His reading is very meaningful, and he sets the point of departure of this duality in Plato. In the case of Socrates, I think this distinction does not work so well. As a pedagogue or philosopher or *philophronein,* Socrates' love for Alcibiades is concerned that he lives a more caring life. Both dimensions seem to be present in his practice. It is not a matter of utility or aim but of meaning and sense. The sense of Socrates' philosophy and pedagogy is that others take care of themselves in their living together. The same argument could be made about Nicias in the *Laches:* in order to live a life that deserves to be lived, Nicias and all the others need to take care of themselves by thinking accurately. So the two possibilities differentiated by Foucault are not unconnected in Socrates, in fact one cannot work without the other. In this sense, I think the *Alcibiades I* and the *Laches* are just stressing two sides of the same philosophical or educational coin for Socrates, although we might suggest that maybe Plato needed to make this distinction. Nor is it a trivial fact that the context of both *dialogues* is the political life of Athens. Both Alcibiades and Nicias are, have been, or will be public figures, men of the city. So I do not see any self-task being suggested by itself or for its own sake, or any private domain disconnected from the public one in these *dialogues,* or in the *Lysis* either. I would still argue that in the case of Socrates, the self and the care of the self are always (or most of the time) living selves, i.e., both individual life and communal life are what Socrates seems to be worried about. The issue that you raise of love of the world, *philokosmos,* is really fascinating and I am not sure about it. I don't know. We might need to study it as it appears in both

Socrates and Isocrates. Also, the issue remains of what it means to live a philosophical life, and its relationship to school. Socrates is once again fascinating here, because he is a pedagogue and philosopher with no institutional school, or whose "school" is *schole*—that is, a formalized experience of free time and space. He says this at the beginning of the *Phaedrus*: to do philosophy with others we need friendship and *schole*. He doesn't meet the others in *schole* to teach or to do philosophy, rather he creates or builds *schole* while philosophizing, or in order to philosophize. My friend Giuseppe Ferraro (2011: 12) says it beautifully: it not that we come to be friends because we do philosophy, but it is because we are friends that we do philosophy. Thus, this enigmatic and impossible figure of Socrates, paradoxical and self-contradictory, creates school (as *schole*) while doing philosophy. Through his pedagogical and philosophical *askesis* he opens life to school and makes school out of life or, to say it more provocatively, makes life a school. Meanwhile, if I'm lost in a Socratic *mania* don't hesitate to tell me! And I'm sure you will be able to help me think through this relationship between philosophical life and school.

JM: Dear Walter, as it has been some time before I could respond, I had to reread what we have written so far. And as is to be expected, there are many things we have touched upon and which would be worthwhile to continue with. I would like to take up only two or three things.

Let me start with Isocrates. I agree with much of what you write about these two texts (including the arrogance issue), and I would also agree that for Isocrates oratory (i.e. a kind of public speech where you are not addressing someone individually, but every-one, so to say) is much more important than for Socrates. I think that this difference is important, in that Isocrates addresses his audience starting from the idea that he can convince them, and as such they are equals; whereas the Socrates of the *Apology* seems to imply the opposite—albeit not at every moment, and of course Isocrates' defence in the *Antidosis* is a fictional one. I also believe that it is important that Isocrates, although he is close to the sophists, writes against them in the sense that he is radical in his conviction that there is no final truth to be gained about human affairs, and that their claims to be able to teach such truth (or wisdom) and to impart happiness are idle and false (what he claims he is speaking is *parrhesia*, again very similar to Socrates—see eg. *Antidosis* 43). Now, I must say that my understanding of the role of Isocrates in thinking about education (and school) is also influenced by the extended commentaries on his life and work by people like Takis Poulakos (1997) and Yun Lee Too (2003), and is not limited to the two texts that we're talking about here. It is clear that different readings are possible (as of course is always the case), but there seems to be an agreement among scholars that Isocrates is in fact himself constantly alternating between a conservative, rather aristocratic stance and a truly democratic one, as well as between a kind of Athenian "nationalism" (and an idea of the superiority of Athens) and a plea for "cosmopolitism".

I don't want to defend Isocrates or imply that he is more "right" than Socrates, but I find it very interesting that he offers (at times and in some parts) a different view of the relationship between philosophy and education. Or to phrase it differently, there are some really interesting elements in his work that help me think not only philosophy as education, but also the role of education as such. It would take much more space than we have to elaborate this (and in fact we might envisage in the future some common seminar where we could enter this discussion), but let me sum up some of the issues.

First, his views on opinion and knowledge are completely contrary to Plato's (and probably closer to at least several of the various "Socrates"). As he writes in "*Against the Sophists*": "those who follow their opinions (*doxai*) live more harmoniously and are more successful than those who claim to have knowledge (*epistèmè*)" *Against the Sophists* 8 (I'm using a recent translation by Mirhady and Too, 2000, but you'll find the other translation below)[1]. This is in line with his emphasis on the need for deliberation within democracy and the importance of opinion in making judgments. The starting point that "it is not in our nature to know in advance what is going to happen" (*Against the Sophists* 2) and therefore study/teaching "cannot make the young ... know what they need to do and through this knowledge ... become happy" (*Against the Sophists* 3). He emphasizes the role of debate and speech (speaking well) time and time again, but "teaching" the young in this context (which is always a "creative activity") is not "like teaching the alphabet": "while the function of letters is unchanging ... the function of words is entirely opposite .... speeches cannot be good unless they reflect the circumstances, propriety and originality ..."(*Against the Sophists* 12–13)[2]. The teaching is therefore not related to *episteme* but is the formation of *doxa* (related to sound judgment, which is creative with respect to the occasion) and this formation is also dependent on the exchange of speeches themselves—on deliberation. "These things require much study and are the work of a brave and imaginative soul. In addition to having the requisite natural ability, the student must learn the forms of speeches and practice their uses. The teacher must go through these aspects as precisely as possible, so that nothing teachable is left out, but as for the rest, he must offer himself as a model [*paradeigma*, and not *basanos* or touchstone—and maybe this is also something we could pursue]" (*Against the Sophists* 17)[3]. So, the first important thing for me is this emphasis on the formation of *doxa*, which implies a recognition of the importance of speech and the exchange of opinions. It means that philosophers cannot transcend or go beyond the realm of opinion (contrary to Plato), and that the philosopher is fundamentally a man of opinion[4]. And this opinion is about the governing of one's household, but also and especially about the commonwealth and the common good—about the affairs of the city: "those who learn and practice what allows them to manage well their own homes and the city's commonwealth—for which one must work hard, engage in philosophy, and do everything necessary" (*Antidosis* 285).

This brings me to the second thing that I consider important: you have to work hard and *do* philosophy, which is "practice and study". It is the importance of the formation of opinion (which enables one to participate) through philosophy, which is in the first place the practice (or exercise—often called "*epimeleia*") and study of words (poetry, history, politics—which are the words not of gods, but of "men") and not the study of (ideal) forms (mathematics, geometry), although Isocrates does accept the latter as a kind of preparatory work (see *Antidosis* 261–8). In this context, it is true that Isocrates also refers to "natural ability", but I think one should not overemphasize this, since at some points it seems to imply not much more than the general statement that one has to be able to speak; and he writes that one can even downplay one's own natural ability—which maybe echoes Rancière's lack of self-respect—see *Antidosis* 244). I agree that there are also other passages where "natural ability" seems to be more than that (e.g. *Antidosis* 138) and even this general statement can be questioned, but I would prefer to point to his recurrent emphasis on "hard work" and "study" (or "labor" and "exercise") which, at the end of the *Antidosis* he also claims to be necessary even for those who seem be "naturally apt". Moreover in 291 he writes: "I marvel at men who felicitate those who are eloquent by nature on being blessed with a noble gift, and yet rail at those who wish to become eloquent, on the ground that they desire an immoral and debasing education. Pray, what that is noble by nature becomes shameful and base when one attains it by effort? We shall find that there is no such thing, but that, on the contrary, we praise, at least in other fields, those who by their own devoted toil are able to acquire some good thing more than we praise those who inherit it from their ancestors" (Perseus translation). And in 292: "For men who have been gifted with eloquence by nature and by fortune, are governed in what they say by chance, and not by any standard of what is best, whereas those who have gained this power by the study of philosophy and by the exercise of reason never speak without weighing their words, and so are less often in error as to a course of action" (Perseus translation). So it seems to me, that Isocrates, although at some moments he seems to point to "nature" and "natural ability", is much more emphasizing the importance of study and practice. And he explicitly calls this a form of "*epimeleia*": in 290 he states that "if one is to govern his youth rightly and worthily and make the proper start in life, he must give more heed ('*epimeleian*') to himself than to his possessions, he must not hasten and seek to rule over others before he has found a master to direct his own thoughts, and he must not take as great pleasure or pride in other advantages as in the good things which spring up in the soul under a liberal education" (*Antidosis* 290—Perseus translation). This is, I think, very close to what Socrates is saying to Alcibiades about "taking care of oneself", but

Isocrates relates this *"epimeleia"* directly to study and practice, and to hard work and labor. And I think that this implies a rupture with the idea of a natural destination and a natural order (the archaic aristocratic order), as there seems to be no privilege either regarding "knowledge"—since there is no such thing when we speak of human affairs—nor regarding study—for if naturally apt in the sense of not being handicapped, everyone can practice and study. If there is superiority it is thanks to "being educated as have been no other people in wisdom (*phronesis*) and in speech (*logous*)" (294). Yun Lee Too (2003) also remarks that the fact that one could also get education/teaching ("free time") by paying implied that the archaic aristocratic order, where only those who by privilege/nature had "free time" could do this, was disrupted. Of course we can also question this, and it is certainly different from Socrates (Plato) who explicitly states that he didn't ask for any money for his teaching, but what is interesting for me is just this disruption of the archaic order and the invention of new ways of dealing with study and practice.

Isocrates emphasizes both teaching (*didaskein*) and care (*epimeleia*), and points to both the possibilities and the limits of teaching. The latter is not about (transmitting) knowledge, but about contributing to the formation of opinion through guiding and sustaining study and practice in order to get to *phronesis* and *eulegein* (speaking well). He thereby acknowledges that judgment and speaking are always part of a "creative process" related to the occasion, and that one needs actual (written or oral) expression in order to "complete" an opinion. The act of writing or speaking well is not just a recording of a thought/opinion which existed before, but its completion—and this always implies a "public/audience". Moreover, teaching does not require us to leave the world of *doxai* to get to an enlightened realm of knowledge (to get out of the cave), but does require us to study that world, and especially the words (and the art of words) in their relation to issues of the common good. I think this is also an important point, because Isocrates is at pains to state again and again that the oratory he is interested in is not related to private affairs and the use of words in the context of juridical disputes, but to public disputes about the common good. Where the sophists mainly taught to sustain individual ambitions and were not concerned with the public good but with private influence and personal gain, and where the sophists were interested in psychological impact, Isocrates was interested in cultivating and deliberating as a practice, not in view of an ideal state, but related to "those public issues which are important and noble and promote human welfare" (*Antidosis* 276).

There are more things that make Isocrates interesting for me, but I can only point to them very briefly. One is that he was actually trying to avoid the tribunal as well as the agora, precisely in order to be able to study and practice (to form opinion). One commentator has remarked that Isocrates offered the "gift of time" to oratory. He did this by taking the words out of their immediate practical embeddedness (when one is defending oneself or accusing in courts, or when one is arguing for a decision in the *boule*) and making them into an object of study (not only listening but reading, commenting) and practice as such, and he did this not only by instauring (maybe one could indeed say inventing) school as a formal frame, but also by making writing a central operation. In fact he himself was mainly writing speeches, not actually delivering them (if he is famous to some extent, it is not because of his oral performances like most of the sophists, but because of his writings), but also his study and practice were directly related to writing (he is the inventor of the school essay), which I think was also a powerful way both to "slow down" (to give time to the words of men, to read and reread) and to "make public"—and as I said before, I think this has also to do with his speeches not being addressed to a particular individual or collection of individuals, but with being public speech. He also is very clear about the fact that the purpose of this study of words is not just to know them and how to use them, but is also related to the formation of a good character (a "gentleman") since "the man who wishes to persuade people will not be negligent as to the matter of character; no, on the contrary, he will apply himself above all to establish a most honorable name among his fellow-citizens; for who does not know that words carry greater conviction when spoken by men of good repute than when spoken by men who live under a cloud, and that the argument which is made by a man's life is of more weight than that which is furnished by words?" (*Antidosis* 278).

I should also say that there are many passages in both texts (and certainly in the first part of the *Antidosis*) where I have plenty of questions and even feel uneasy; however, as I have already said, my point is not to enter into a debate about a choice between Socrates and Isocrates, but rather that if we seek to understand "school" and to think of education and philosophy starting from the school, there are very interesting elements to find in Isocrates. These may be closer than I am acknowledging to the ones you mention in relation to Socrates, but they are surely very different from Plato.

Now leaving Isocrates behind for the moment, let me again take up one of the main concerns we have been engaged in until now: the relation/distinction between philosophy and education (philosophy and/or/of/with/as/through ... education). In this context, you mentioned at the very beginning of our "double dialogue with ourselves" (you see, from the moment I try to write something all kinds of new but related issues pop up such as the kind of exercise we both are engaged in and how we might conceive of it (I first thought to write "conversation", but is that a good word, is it in itself philosophy?) And so on....—you mentioned that we might focus on "the figure of the professor of philosophy, who in a sense is in between philosophy and education and practices philosophy as education". You referred to Foucault inscribing himself in the tradition inaugurated by Socrates, in which the professor of philosophy occupies a singular and paradoxical position: he takes care of himself by not taking care *ipso facto* of himself but by taking care that all the others take care of themselves. Now what I was wondering was whether you could ever separate "being a philosopher or philosophizing as act" from "being a teacher/professor/master" in some way or other. In fact I have been rereading some other texts (Kant, Lyotard, Stiegler), which might be helpful here. Indeed, they all seem to imply that philosophy cannot be separated from teaching (or instruction). Stiegler (2008, chapter 7), who refers to the beginning of Plato's *Hippias Minor*, 363a, even states *"la première question que pose la philosophie, ..., ce n'est pas l'être, ... c'est l'enseignement"* and adds *"l'enseignement n'est pas simplement la première question de la philosophie: c'est la* pratique *de la philosophie"* (2008: 195–6). And Kant, in the context of his discussion of the difference between the "scholastic concept of philosophy" and the "cosmic concept of philosophy" (in the last part of the *Critique of Pure Reason*) states that you cannot learn philosophy but only learn to philosophize, and that the cosmic concept has always formed the real foundation of that which has been given the title of philosophy. He writes: "The mathematician, the natural philosopher, and the logician, however successful the former two may have been in their advances in the field of rational knowledge are yet only artificers in the field of reason. There is a teacher, [conceived] in the ideal that sets them their tasks, and employs them as instruments, to further the essential ends of human reason. Him alone we must call philosopher" (A839/B867). His idea is that the ideal of the philosopher implies the teacher as the one who seeks to further the essential ends of humanity. So time and again we find the relation between the philosopher and the teacher (of philosophy?), and I am wondering more and more how exactly to understand this relationship. Can you be a philosopher without teaching? Can you philosophize without teaching? In his little book *Le Postmoderne expliqué aux enfants* Lyotard (1988) also encloses an *"Adresse au sujet du cours philosophique"*, in which he states that "philosophy" is always only "in act" (*"en acte"*) and has to be opposed to any capacity/power (*"puissance"*). He writes: *"Je te confesse qu'éduquer et instruire ne me semblent ni plus ni moins des « actes philosophiques » que banqueter ou armer un navire"*. Here he seems to imply that every act can be a philosophical act, but if I try to understand what he means by *"actes philosophiques"* it seems to me that these are philosophical because they are educational (that is forming, in the sense of problematizing). Thus he argues, *"À première vue, donc, on n'aperçoit pas de différence de nature entre philosopher et enseigner la philosophie"*.

Maybe you could help me out here? I've always had the impression that being a teacher is considered an additional feature of the philosopher (also implying, with Kant, that one is first enlightened through philosophy, then teaches), but maybe this is wrong—maybe we should think about teaching as an essential feature of philosophy in the sense that you cannot philosophize without teaching (in the minimal sense of exposing your knowledge and skills)?

I must confess that I am really confused about this matter, just as I am confused about the relation between philosophy and friendship. Indeed, when thinking from another angle about the relation between philosophy and education, and adhering to the oft-mentioned idea that there is no philosophy without friends, I was wondering how that can be combined with "childhood" and "children": can you say that there is no education without friends? Can we (as teachers) be friends who philosophize with children? And of course, dear Walter, I am confident that, as you are at home in "philosophy with children" (if that is an acceptable description), that you can help me out here.

Excuse me for this probably very disappointing finish, but I fear that I have already created too much confusion, such that a different perspective is needed to regain direction in our reciprocal writing.

WOK: Dear Jan, the time you took to respond is consistent with such a strong and thoughtful intervention. Thank you very much for the opportunity to share in your thinking in such a vivid way. Thank you so much also for letting me see a little more clearly why you find Isocrates so interesting. And thank you for the suggestion that we share a seminar on these issues. It would be a privilege and an opportunity to continue thinking together. Concerning Isocrates I can only say that I feel compelled to read him and his commentators more carefully. His stress on *doxa*, his conception of philosophy and/or education as study and practice, and his invention of new ways of study and practice as well—all this sounds fascinating and promising. His description of the teacher as a model or "paradigm" reminds me of Socrates' use of the same word in the *Apology* (23b) to refer to the way the Oracle has chosen him as representative of a kind of relationship to human knowledge: the wise man, he discovers through her choice, is the one who acknowledges that no one is really wise. This is why Socrates is a paradigm. It is interesting among other things because the context seems to be a pedagogical one; that is, the Oracle has taught the Athenians, through the example of Socrates, what it means to be truly wise. It is also interesting in that, as far as I remember, no distinction is present in the *Apology* between different sorts of knowledge, such as *doxa* and *episteme*. There is, however, still something in your presentation of Isocrates that does not convince me. Because he addresses his audience starting from the idea that he can convince them, I am not sure that he considers them as equals. I think that this is related to one of the interesting implications of Rancière's *The Ignorant Schoolmaster*: that a good part of the history of pedagogy could be considered to be based on the practice of stultification, as much on the part of those teachers who rely on their capacity to convince their students of something as not. But I really need to read more of Isocrates to be able to offer any kind of serious argument about his practice. And you have convinced me that that in order to understand "school" and to think of education and philosophy as practices starting from school, there are very interesting elements to be found in

Isocrates. The last two issues you pose are really fascinating and complex. I am tempted not to separate teaching from philosophizing—it doesn't make me any more comfortable to see the teacher as an additional feature of the philosopher than it does to see philosophizing as an additional feature of a teacher. I would not say it is wrong, but I would say that it does not recognize the power (for thinking and practice) that can be derived from the image of the philosopher-teacher or the teacher-philosopher. To say it in another way, a teacher who does not philosophize is not (and here the word is really difficult!) a true, real or genuine teacher any more than a philosopher who does not teach is not a true, real or accurate philosopher. As you know philosophy and education are multiplicities, and there are many ways to conceive of them and their relationship. In fact, if we go to the canonical history of philosophy we might find many philosophers who not only did not teach, but who considered teaching to be something very far from philosophy; nor would I say that they are wrong or that they are not philosophers because of that. But I would say that they are not truly, really, interestingly philosophers, if we think "philosopher" in a sense that we would certainly need to be more precise. And the same could be said of the history of pedagogy. Certainly a more thorough history of philosophy as education and a history of education as philosophy needs to be written, but this seems like a Sisyphean task. Anyway, there are so many elements here, and I thank you for the ones you have offered. The three examples you propose (Kant, Lyotard and Stiegler) are very meaningful, and it seems pretty clear to me from our conversation that we are now in a position to begin sketching out that history, at least from Isocrates and Socrates on. And let me suggest to you that even though he would not count as one of our favorites, I think Plato should also have a place in that history of philosophy as education or education as philosophy. Let me justify this inclusion—even though I can well imagine your expression of astonishment on reading these words—or let me try. Let's hypothesize that this history of philosophy as education was initiated by Isocrates and Socrates (and maybe some others too). And it seems to me that Plato was very dissatisfied with these philosophers/educators in the way their practice of philosophy/education contributed to the political crisis of Athens. The case of Socrates seems clear, and many of Plato's *dialogues* combine this mixture of admiration and complaint that Plato feels for his master. In addition, many commentators testify to finding Isocrates behind lots of the *dialogues*. *The Republic* is a clear example of this: philosophers (educators) are considered useless or perverse and they need to be resituated as philosopher-kings, as stated in book VII. Maybe Socrates is a good image of the inutility of the philosopher, while Isocrates is an example of one of its dangerous characters. In any case, the allegory of the cave ends with quite an antithesis to what Socrates affirms in the *Apology*. In the latter, Socrates is happy not to have taken part in the political affairs of the city, because if he had done so he would have been killed many years before.

In *The Republic,* Socrates asserts that the city will not find its true form until the king philosophizes or the philosophers govern. In other words, while for the Socrates of the *Apology* there is a hostile opposition between the practice of philosophy and political life, for the Socrates (Plato) of *The Republic* the philosopher can only fulfill his practice as a politician. And we might include Isocrates in this triangle as someone who, like Socrates, conceived of philosophy as a practice, so in a sense was opposed to Plato, but took a precise place in political life, as Plato—the disciple of Socrates— did. So that if both Socrates and Isocrates conceived of philosophy as practice (again, very differently one from the other), both Isocrates and Plato considered philosophy to have its place in political life. This is precisely what Calicles criticizes about Socrates in Plato's *Gorgias* (485d–486b) arguing that philosophy is good to practice in childhood, but not when one enters political life. And it is worth noticing that, in *The Republic,* the philosopher has no chance *not* to do what he is supposed to do: given that he has been educated by the city, he will come back to educate the whole city by governing it, whether willingly or forced to do so. So that for Plato, the philosopher is at the same time an educator and a politician, and cannot be a true philosopher without being both. We can disagree about how he considers each of these—philosophy as knowledge of the forms, pedagogy as liberation from the cave, and politics as an aristocracy in which everyone fulfills their natural function—but the relationship between the three remains very close, and in this respect Isocrates seems closer to Plato than Socrates, in that he considers philosophy as educational to be essential for political aims. Of course both seem to conceive of the nature of philosophy as education, but to conceive of its political aims very differently, as you have pointed out: Isocrates identifies philosophy as the study and practice of *doxa* in favor of opinion, judgment and deliberation within a democratic context, while Plato conceives of philosophy/education as true theoretical knowledge (episteme) in the context of an aristocratic order. What I am trying to suggest here, Jan, is that it could be there is not only one but several histories of philosophy as education, and that we need to consider philosophy, not only as education but as practice, and as occupying a given location in relation to the political order. If we consider philosophy as practice, one name that could play an interesting role in that history is Matthew Lipman, the creator of what he called "philosophy for children". Lipman argued that the doing of philosophy, philosophical praxis, was essential to educational experience because of the way, in his words, it embodied "reasonableness". Given that philosophy and education share reasonableness as the same goal, he concludes "all true philosophy is educational and all true education is philosophical" (1988: 43). Like Isocrates, he identified the practice of educational philosophy as essential to the development of the judgement of democratic citizens. From this side of the ocean another precious name in that history is Simón Rodríguez, the inventor of popular education in

Latin America. In fact, Jan, there seem to be names everywhere! We might need to (re)read Montaigne, Spinoza, and so many others. In any case, it seems to me that (re)writing the history of philosophy/education as practice requires the (re)writing not only of its practical history, but also of its relationship to politics (democracy), and from that perspective Isocrates and Socrates seem to inaugurate two opposite routes. Too ambitious for a seminar?! One other figure who could contribute to questioning this enterprise is Derrida, especially his *Du droit à la philosophie* (1990). Many of what he calls "Les antinomies de la discipline philosophique" touch on our question. See for example the third antinomy: "*D'une part, nous nous sentons en droit d'exiger que la recherche ou le questionnement philosophiques ne soient jamais dissociés de l'enseignement. (…) Mais d'autre part, nous nous sentons aussi autorisés à rappeler que, peut-être pour l'essentiel, quelque chose de la philosophie ne se limite pas, ne s'est pas toujours limité à des actes d'enseignement, à des événements scolaires, à ses structures institutionelles, voire à la discipline philosophique elle-même. Celle-ci peut toujours être débordée, parfois provoquée par de l'inenseignable. Peut-être doit-elle se plier à enseigner l'inenseignable, à se produire en renonçant à elle-même, en excédant sa propre identité*" (1990: 518). Even though it might seem challenging, I very much like this passage and do consider that the task of philosophy is to teach the unteachable. And we could write a parallel antinomy, centred on education, affirming that on the one hand we might demand that every dimension of education should be submitted to philosophy, to philosophical experience; but that on the other hand there must be something essentially educative that is not subject to philosophy. Education might then be understood as philosophizing the unphilosophizable, thinking the unthinkable. So once again, philosophy and education are looking very much alike—in fact maybe this is where we are now in our dialogical journey. Hopefully, dear Jan, the difficulties we are facing in clearly thinking what we are trying to think have to do with the antinomic character of the relationship under discussion. Indeed, far from inhibiting thinking, this condition makes it even more necessary to continue looking for its place. Perhaps, like Heraclitus, we need to expect the unexpectable. And yes, I have been engaged in taking the relationship between childhood and philosophy seriously for at least the last 20 years. At the beginning I was much influenced by Matthew Lipman, and since then I've gradually tried to develop my own perspectives on the field, which includes a problematization of the idea of childhood and a move from a chronological approach to a more aionic one—one that includes children but is not limited to them. While *chronos* is the time of institutions, of school and psychology, *aion* is the time of *schole*, thinking and friendship. If *chronos* is the time of teaching the institutionalized discipline of philosophy, *aion* is the time of philosophy as education. So in this sense the practice of doing philosophy with children is a practice of making *schole*, making free-time, aionic time out of the chronological time of school. Through philosophizing with chronological children in pedagogical institutions, I have been moved to try to think an aionic childhood of philosophy as education, or a childlike education through the experience of philosophy. It is in this sense that I think friendship is a condition of philosophy. In my previous post I referred to Giuseppe's Ferrari inversion of the etymology of philosophy (wisdom of friendship or love instead of love of wisdom). For a certain Socrates, this is the only thing philosophy can know, it is in fact the only thing Socrates declares himself wise about (*ta erotica, Symposium* 177d). What I mean is that if there is something a philosopher can know about beyond his or her own lack of knowledge, it is about *philia*, because this emerges from the affirmative dimension of ignorance: while professing to not-knowing, the philosopher as educator is passionate about knowing, is a friend of knowing, is in love with knowing. So friendship seems to be at the core of philosophy as education, just as I feel we have practiced in this dialogue. Don't you think so, dear Jan?

JM: Dear Walter, although we have, of course, not solved any issue and have reached no end, I think we have taken a wonderful path, and have come to a point where we might look for a different way to continue our walk through (some history of) philosophy and/or of education. I like the remarks you make about the "triangle" between Plato, Socrates and Isocrates very much, especially the implication for politics that you are suggesting. I think we could take these remarks as a starting point for a seminar, symposium or colloquium; and since the second option seems also to offer the occasion for some commoning of "food" not limited to food for thought, we might consider that one? What if we were to arrange it for sometime and somewhere in the coming months? Meanwhile, let me make a very brief last comment related to this element of "politics" in our musings, as I think it might help us further explore the relationship between philosophy and education, and to avoid the danger of what I would call an "ethical" or even "moral" colonization of the practice and theory of education (which, it could be, is to some extent related to our philosophical inheritance). At the beginning of our exchange you wrote that what Socrates is doing is to provoke "the impossibility of continuing to live as one was living before", and I have been relating that to Rilke's commandment that emerges from out of the stone torso: "you must change your life". Well, let me suggest that this "imperative to change" and the discourse about change more generally (and maybe also about "transformation"), to which I myself am also attracted time and again, is indeed always leading us towards such an ethically (morally) "colonized" understanding of education, in which "changing your life" is always involved, and therefore always includes a kind of judgment as its starting point (i.e., that something is in whatever way "wrong" or "insufficient" or in need of "light" or "clarity", and that change is wanted, needed, looked for, aspired to, suggested, required, desirable. But what if education is not about change, at least not in its first impulse, or to say it more precisely: of course change occurs or can occur and is involved in the process of education, and is probably even its result, but education is first of all about "adding" ("giving", "offering"—"receiving") something—an adding which is a form of enabling and that is not based on an assumption or attribution or revelation of "lack" (however we understand "lack") and not a simple accumulation. Maybe this could be related to the wonderful thing you've just wrote about "philosophizing" as "creating school" or "making school while doing philosophy", because it seems to imply clearly that both (philosophizing and making school) are not the same, that you can philosophize without "making school" and that "school" is adding something—and that "thing", I would suggest, is added by the gift of time. Turning to politics, although it could lead us into other versions of "colonization", might help us to explore the issue of "things" or of "world", an issue we have already touched upon before. Let me conclude on my side by expressing my profound gratitude for this most wonderful experience and the chance you gave me to engage in this great "correspondence", which I think, upon a suggestion made here in Leuven by Tim Ingold, is the best word for it. Co-responding *with* each other, but also and for sure *with* philosophy and/or education.

WOK: "the adding of some thing by the gift of time"—what a nice and strong way of saying what education (and/or philosophy?!) is about! I very much agree with your comments about the risky and colonizing dimension of the "lack-change" discourse, and I think you have stated very clearly what seems to be our path for continuing to think a politically non-colonizing education and/or philosophy. And as I write this, I remember another risk and I am tempted to write "a non-colonizing and (at the same time) non-conservative education". I am aware that this word "conservative" needs more careful consideration, but I am trying to focus our attention on a path that gives origin to philosophy and/or education. Let me try to put it more clearly. Usually, the feelings associated with the origin of philosophy are wonder, doubt, and perplexity, and the consciousness of being lost (as stated, for example, by Jaspers, 1959). But I also think that dissatisfaction or discontent with our common world, with the way we live and think and relate in common or in community is a feeling crucial to the birth of philosophy as school—to doing school through philosophy or to philosophizing as education. And if it is true that this originary impulse has given place to a politically colonizing, dominating discourse in education and philosophy, it is also true that it might find its place as an origin of a non-colonizing philosophy as education. There is a lot to think about dear Jan, and I really thank you for such a wonderful opportunity of co-respondence, as Tim Ingold has magnificently worded it. And thank you for adding, offering, and giving birth in me to a new word, "commoning"—such a nice way of indicating the act of putting something into a common space, which in a sense symbolizes what philosophy as/and education is about. In fact it brings us back (or forth) to Heraclitus in at least a couple of senses (in fact we might need to go back to a little before Socrates, Plato and Isocrates!), particularly his emphasis—with words like *xynos* and *koinos*—on the common as a mark of the world. And I now remember a few more words from Heraclitus, with which I will finish: first, his brilliant fragment 103, "In a circle, beginning and end are common (*xynon*)" (2001, translation M. Marcovich), which makes me feel that the ending of this correspondence is also the beginning of other, new correspondences; and second, the old proverb *"koina ta ton philon"* (common, things from friends), which in a sense symbolizes not only our correspondence, but what education as/and philosophy is about: a unique experience emerging through the words of friends who are noticing, realizing, and giving full attention to the world in common, to the common life. That's probably why it is so difficult to end a correspondence like this, because in a sense it is like ending a path in thinking—unless we realize that an end is always a beginning in our commoning the world. Looking forward to the symposium!!!

Notes

1 "that those who follow their judgements are more consistent and more successful than those who profess to have exact knowledge"
2 "For, excepting these teachers, who does not know that the art of using letters remains fixed and unchanged, that we continually and invariably use the same letters for the same purposes, while exactly the reverse is true of the art of discourse…. that oratory is good only if it has the qualities of fitness for the occasion, propriety of style, and originality of treatment."
3 "These things, I hold, require much study and are the task of a vigorous and imaginative mind: for this, the student must not only have the requisite aptitude but he must learn, the different kinds of discourse and practise himself in their use; and the teacher, for his part, must so expound the principles of the art with the utmost possible exactness as to leave out nothing that can be taught, and, for the rest, he must in himself set such an example of oratory."
4 Moreover, Isocrates was close to the sophists where they were materialistic, refuting mythical explanations–see also his defense of Aanaxagoras and Damon in *Antidosis* (235).

Bibliography

Arendt, H. (1958) "The Crisis in Education", in *Between Past and Future*. New York: Penguin Classics.
Derrida, J. (1990) *Du droit à la philosophie*. Paris: Gallimard.
———. (1997) *De l'hospitalité*. Anne Dufourmantelle invite Jacques Derrida à répondre. Paris: Calmann-Lévy.
———. (2000) 'La pharmacie de Platon' in Platon, *Phèdre*. Trans. L. Brisson. Paris: GF-Flammarion, pp 255–403.
Ferraro, G. (2011) *La scuola dei sentimenti*. Napoli: Filema.
Foucault, M. *L'herméneutique du sujet*. Cours au Collège de France, 1981-1982. Paris: Gallimard; Seuil, 2001.

————. *Le courage de la vérité. Le gouvernement de soi et des autres II.* Cours au Collège de France, 1983-1984. Paris: Gallimard; Seuil, 2009.

Hadot, P. (1993) *Exercices spirituels et philosophie antique.* Paris: Albin Michel.

Heraclitus (2001) *Heraclitus,* ed. Miroslav Marcovich. Sankt Augustin: Academia Verlag.

Isocrates (2000) *Against the Sophists.* Engl. Trans. Mirhady and Too. Austin: University of Texas Press.

Jaspers, K. (1959) *Introduction to Philosophy.* New Haven: Yale University Press.

Kant, I. (1929) *Critique of Pure Reason.* Trans. Norman Kemp Smith. London: Macmillan.

Lee Too, J. (2003) *The Pedagogical Contract.* Ann Arbor: University of Michigan Press.

Liddell, H. and Scott, R. (1966) *A Greek English Lexicon.* Oxford: Clarendon Press.

Lipman, M. (1988) *Philosophy Goes to School.* Philadelphia: Temple University Press.

Lyotard, J.-F. (1988) *Le Postmoderne expliqué aux enfants.* Paris: Gallimard.

Plato (1990) *Platonis Opera,* ed. John Burnet. Oxford: Oxford University Press. *The Dialogues of Plato.* Trans. B. Jowett. New York: Oxford University Press, 1989.

Poulakis, T. (1997) *Speaking for the Polis. Isocrates' Rhetorical Education.* Columbia: University of South Carolina Press.

Rancière, J. (1987) *Le maître ignorant.* Paris: Fayard.

Rilke, R. M. (1908) "Archaïscher Torso Apollos", in *Der Neuen Gedichte Anderer Teil.* Leipzig: Insel Verlag.

Rodríguez, S. (2001a) *Obra Completa.* Tomos I-II. Caracas: Presidencia de la República.

Sloterdijk, P. (2013) *You Must Change Your Life.* Cambridge: Polity Press.

Stiegler, B. (2008) *Prendre soin, de la jeunesse et des générations.* Paris: Flammarion. Engl. Trans.: *Taking Care of Youth and the Generations.* Stanford: Stanford University Press, 2010.

Yun Lee Too (2003) *The Pedagogical Contract.* Ann Arbor: The University of Michigan Press.

Index